CW00493756

The Power of Comparison

Robert Prior was a professional Economist for more than 20 years, working in London and, subsequently, in Singapore. Returning to the UK in 2014, he completed a number of psychology courses including a Certificate of Higher Education. He also obtained a Diploma in Cognitive Behavioural Therapy and is a registered CBT therapist. He has bachelor's and master's degrees from the University of Warwick.

The Power of Comparison

A Manual For Better Living

Robert Prior

To my (incomparable) parents

Contents

PART 1

Comparisons & 'The Self'

PART 2

Comparisons in 'External' Situations

Acknowledgements

I am indebted to my son, Ben, for his considerable help with the design of the cover and production of all the images inside the book. The pictures on the front and back cover are credited to Erik Lam and Eric Isselee respectively.

I have made use of many academic studies in this book, the researchers and authors of which I am extremely grateful to.

With thanks also to my other son, Alex, for his invaluable assistance and to those that have read the various drafts and made helpful suggestions, including my wife, Angela, and parents. Any remaining mistakes are of course mine.

In the land of the blind, the one-eyed man is king

Credited to Desiderius Erasmus, Dutch Humanist and Scholar (1466-1536)

Introduction

It's **All** Relative

Have a quick look at the images below and decide which of the two central circles, A or B, is the biggest.

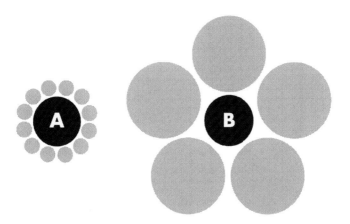

The chances are that you chose A or, if you know this trick, neither. The correct answer is B! Circle A only appears to be bigger because we can't help but compare the size of A and B to the other circles surrounding them. If those reference points are removed, as they are overleaf, it's apparent that B is (marginally) bigger than A. This is a variant of the Ebbinghaus illusion and has huge relevance to our everyday lives.

Comparisons influence how we see ourselves...

Let me ask you a question: *how clever are you?*

Your answer will be determined by how clever you perceive yourself to be relative to an average of some sort. For example, you might know that you have an IQ of 110 and the UK average is 100, leading you to conclude that you're 'quite clever'.

But if you don't believe an IQ test is a good measure of cleverness, you don't know your IQ and/or you're unaware of the UK average you'll have to compare yourself in some other way: probably against people with whom you spend most time. As a result, if you generally mix with extremely smart individuals, there's a good chance you'll conclude that you're not particularly bright. If, however, the opposite is true, you may well decide that you're clever. The point is, your actual cleverness is the same in both cases but your *perception* of how smart you are is very different.

This effect was demonstrated in a US study, where pupils' assessment of their academic ability was found to be lower in highly selective schools than in less selective ones, adjusting for their actual ability.[1] Why? Because they compared themselves with their fellow students rather than a wider student population. Consequently, pupils in the elite schools were harder on themselves than those with the same 'intelligence' who happened to attend other schools.

Profound practical implications often follow as a result of such judgements. Let's say we're confronted with a difficult mental challenge. The chance of us solving the task will be a lot higher if we perceive ourselves to be clever rather than if we're convinced we're incompetent. In other words, it's not just how clever we really are that determines how likely we are to succeed but, what could be termed, our 'self-cleverness-perception'.

Wanting to test the impact of feelings of inferiority on problem solving abilities, a psychologist presented students with a timed test, informing them that, on average, their peers finished it in one-fifth of the time it actually took them. He then rang a bell at that spurious moment and watched how incompetence set in as the students concluded that they were much worse than most.[2]

As another way of illustrating how important comparisons are in dictating how we perceive ourselves, assume that you're the first human to land on another inhabited planet. An alien, who, conveniently, speaks your language, asks, 'How clever are you?' You might answer this question by saying something like, 'Well, from where I come from, most people say I'm smart.' The trouble is this means precisely nothing to the alien who hasn't met anybody else from your planet. He then enquires, 'How strong are you? Are you good at drawing? Do you find it easy to fix things?'

You realise that you have no way of providing meaningful answers to any of the alien's questions. But then you have a brainwave. 'Let's have an arm wrestle and we can test how strong I am.' 'We can both draw a picture of that rock over there and see which you think is best. After that, we could time how long it takes each other to mend something.'

Having completed the tasks, the two of you conclude that the alien is both stronger and better at fixing the item than you but not as good at drawing. By making comparisons you've provided answers that the alien can understand, while also beginning to see how *you* fit into this new world. You begin to believe that you're not that strong or good at fixing things but can at least draw quite well.

The next day, the alien takes you to meet three of his friends and politely requests that you each draw a picture of the landscape. Unbeknown to you he has selected the best artists on the planet and it turns out that your drawing is by far the worst. You decide that you're not particularly good at drawing after all. In fact, with your confidence dented, you start to think that the vast majority of aliens are superior to you in most or all respects. After several similar experiences, you may even come to conclude that you're 'useless' and it's best not to do very much at all for fear of being 'found out'.

In many ways, your experience in this thought-experiment is similar to that of a maturing infant, child and adolescent on planet earth. Given that when we enter the world we're desirous to explore it and find out about ourselves in the process, we're also hard-wired to make comparisons and seek feedback. Our self-image (how we see ourselves) and self-esteem (what we think about ourselves) will be heavily influenced by the results of these comparisons and the reactions we glean from others. If the comparisons are consistently distorted in some way then the same may be true of how we feel about ourselves and, therefore, how we perform and behave.

Relating this to the earlier pictures, if we perceive ourselves to be 'big' relative to those around us (circle A), we're in danger of feeling and acting in a superior way. If, however, we think we're comparatively 'small' (circle B), then we may feel inferior. It all depends on who we happen to compare ourselves with. The words 'big' and 'small' here could relate to almost anything from our physical height to our ability to play chess to our qualities as a school teacher.

...and just about everything else

Our inbuilt obsession with comparisons doesn't just affect how we see ourselves but how we assess everything around us. Like me, you may have replaced your old car with a much better version, convincing yourself that fellow road users are looking on with envy as you proudly take it for a first spin. You park it close to several other vehicles that are not as smart as yours and turn to admire your purchase as you walk away. But just as you do so a brand new sports car pulls up. In that split second, your car is transformed from a highly desirable vehicle to something far more mediocre. And to make matters worse you've been spotted by a passer-by who, helpfully, points out your predicament!

Have you noticed what happens when you redecorate a room? As if by magic, the visual appeal of the furniture in that room and the appearance of other rooms seems to deteriorate, pressurising you into making additional improvements. Having hired somebody for a job who hasn't worked out well, have you then searched for a replacement with the polar opposite characteristics only to be disappointed by that person as well? Maybe you've felt compelled to purchase shares in a company simply because others have made massive 'paper' profits from the same investment? You later regretted the decision. Perhaps you've been impressed by a footballer during the World Cup only to be surprised by his poor performances after he was bought by the club you support? Or you've bought an item because it's price was heavily reduced but subsequently discovered you could have got it cheaper elsewhere?

These are all examples of the powerful influence comparisons can have and how they can throw us off course as we go about our everyday lives.

Better comparisons for a better life

In virtually every aspect of our lives, what we think, the way we feel, how we behave and the conclusions we reach are affected by the specific comparisons we make - if we had used different comparisons the outcomes may also have been different. This isn't necessarily a problem *if* the comparisons are suitable. The trouble is they're often highly inappropriate, leading us to make mental, emotional and behavioural mistakes. At worst, they can completely blight our lives. This book is about how we can make better comparisons to improve our well-being and decision making. It's split into two parts.

In the first, I concentrate on 'The Self' - the comparisons that affect the way we see and think about ourselves. I discuss the sort of comparisons we make and their effects, explore the role of social media, consider what our 'Target-Selves' may look like and how we can progress towards it through our thoughts and deeds. I also consider how to deal better with failure, make habits of our new thoughts and underpin our self-worth. The second part concerns the comparisons we use to assess items external to ourselves when buying, living, working, playing (sport) or investing. We learn how to avoid common pitfalls and arrive at more appropriate judgements, mastering the many tricks of the (comparison) trade in the process.

Focused as I am on comparisons, I'm aware that you, as readers, will inevitably compare the two parts of the book, probably determining that one will be more useful than the other. Nevertheless, I hope you'll have the time and inclination to read both.

PART 1

COMPARISONS & 'THE SELF'

Chapter 1

Why Comparisons Matter

Born to compare...

'My life is so much worse than hers,' 'I'm not as good-looking as he is,' 'I'm better than everybody else on this team' are all examples of social comparisons - the process of thinking about other people in relation to ourselves.[1] According to developmental psychologists we've usually acquired the ability to compare before we can even talk or walk and continue to make comparisons for the rest of our days. Some of us are more active comparers than others, while there will also be periods in our lives when we're more inclined to make comparisons. But, like it or not, we all compare and generally do so automatically.

So what is it that compels us to compare ourselves with others as frequently as we do? We have many motives...

➤ As Leon Festinger - the father of 'Social Comparison Theory', that underpins the academic work in this area – explained *'There exists, in the human organism, a drive to evaluate his opinions and his abilities.'*[2] By so doing, we can understand more about who we are and the (relative) strengths and weaknesses we possess. We could decide, for example, 'I'm better than most of my classmates at writing, but worse than them at music. Therefore I'm not going to volunteer to do a solo at the school concert next month but will write something for the school magazine instead.'

➤ Linked to this, our comparisons help keep us alive! We might think, 'I've never seen or heard about a human being flying without the use of specially designed equipment. I better not give it a go' or 'I'm not as strong or fast as that wild animal. I should get back to safety.'

➤ Social comparisons also tell us how to fit into society or how not to, if we so choose! 'I shouldn't start shouting in this ceremony as nobody else is. Most people don't walk around the office in bare feet, so I won't either.'

➤ They help us establish empathy. By making so-called *downward* comparisons with others - comparisons with those whom we perceive to be worse-off than ourselves - we're able to gain a better understanding of their situation and how they're feeling. 'Unlike me, Jack is unwell today and needs my help and understanding.'

➤ *Upward* comparisons - comparisons with those we perceive to be better than us - can create motivation to improve as well as providing the potential means to do so: we can learn from the success of others. 'I want to be as good at Pool as Rachel. She's told me that she practises for at least an hour a day, so I'm going to do the same and see where that gets me.'

➤ Comparisons between our current-selves and a vision of our future-selves can do the same thing. 'Given that I want to be a well-known journalist in a few years I should contact the local newspaper and offer to write some articles for them.'

> ➤ Comparisons with our past-selves - perceptions of what we used to be like - are an important means of determining how we're progressing in life. 'I can run a lot further than I could do a month ago. I'm going to keep stretching myself.' 'Now that I'm a lot older I won't be able to lift the same weights that I could before and should take it easy.'

...and to be compared

The social comparisons *we* make aren't the only ones that influence our thoughts and deeds. It follows that if we're comparing ourselves with others, then others must be comparing themselves with us. While we'll be oblivious to most of these, we'll no doubt be aware of some. A friend may tell us, for example, 'I know much more than you about the history of the US, although you're better informed than me about British politics.'

Third parties also make comparisons that involve us. A classmate could suggest, 'You're a much slower runner than Richard, while Sarah is a lot better than you at singing. I don't know anybody who swims as well as you, however.'

Alternatively, somebody may simply say, 'You're really smart.' Although this isn't such an obvious comparison, it implicitly involves one. The person commenting and, more importantly, the individual it's directed towards must bring to mind another person or group of people to make sense of it.

Possible pitfalls

Social comparisons are vital to our lives and the way we live them. They bring meaning, letting us understand more about the world around us and how we're placed within it. The problems come when they provide the 'wrong' meaning or a harmful one, potentially creating issues for our mental health. Two issues are important here.

Misleading comparisons

Ideally, everyone would make perfectly accurate and completely appropriate comparisons all of the time. The reality is, of course, very different. We neither have the ability, time nor inclination to do this in the vast majority of situations, particularly when no simple objective means of comparison, such as an IQ test, exists. So how do we solve this problem? Writing in 2011, three academic psychologists argued...

'Instead of engaging in the arduous and often impossible task of finding the most diagnostic standard, one may simply compare with those standards that one routinely uses for comparison.'[3]

Put simply, because our need for mental efficiency trumps our desire to make accurate comparisons, we take a short cut - comparing ourselves with the individual(s) with whom it's easiest to do so. Early in life this is likely to be a sibling and/or contemporary. As we grow older it could be a work colleague or neighbour. But while the target(s) of our comparisons may change, there's always going to be an element of luck whether the person is appropriate or not.

Take a situation when somebody's easiest target for comparisons happens to be younger and less able than themselves. Most of their comparisons will lead them to believe that they're more capable than that individual. Meanwhile, by continually making upward comparisons, the other person could reach precisely the opposite conclusion.

Inappropriate reactions

None of this need matter *if* those involved in the comparisons react appropriately to the results. Sadly, however, this is not always the case. The older individual in my example could easily conclude that they're 'better' than the younger one. And with their sense of ascendancy possibly growing into feelings of general superiority they might end up thinking, 'I'm not just better than him but everyone else as well.' Meanwhile, the younger person may decide that not only are they inferior to the older individual but most people they encounter. Both parties could be fully aware that their comparisons are distorted and yet continue to think unhelpful thoughts, particularly if they have become a habit.

Even if we always used appropriate comparisons and were able to achieve a truly accurate perception of ourselves, the results of our comparisons could still affect our psychological well-being. We might correctly conclude that we're 'rubbish at tennis', for instance, adding it to the 'long list of things we're bad at', instead of shrugging off the results of the comparisons or deciding to work at our game. Alternatively, having made sensible comparisons, we could decide that we're a 'brilliant presenter', leading us to be overconfident and make disparaging remarks about our work colleagues rather than offering helpful advice.

Whether we react appropriately to our comparisons will depend on several factors, including the role played by third parties. Parents could encourage a younger child not to compare themselves with an older brother or sister, explaining that this is unfair on them, for example. They might do the same for the older sibling as well. If, however, they were to undermine the younger child and bolster the elder one, this would only serve to reinforce the impressions the children may already have established about themselves. Our underlying level of self-worth is also important here. Being resilient to the negative implications of upward comparisons and the self-affirming effects of downward ones will stand us in better stead.

In brief

It's easy to see how the combination of our natural desire to make comparisons and our need for speed can lead us to compare ourselves with the wrong people. If we then accept the outcome of these comparisons, as we're prone to do, we can end up with very inaccurate impressions of ourselves, possibly harming our psychological well-being in the process. This is made more likely when third parties reinforce our incorrect conclusions. Even accurate impressions of where we stand relative to appropriate others may have undesirable effects depending on how we react to the results.

This at least is the theory. But is there any hard evidence to suggest that social comparisons have *meaningful* effects on our mental health? And, if so, what are they? I look at this next.

Chapter 2

Exploring the Effects

As we journey through life, we're involved in vast quantities of comparisons with a huge array of different people. Some of them will be favourable and some unfavourable; some helpful and some unhelpful; some kind and some unkind; and some considered and some ill-considered. At the same time, many other factors affecting our psychological condition will also be at play, further complicating the picture. Not surprisingly, therefore, it's very challenging to pinpoint the precise effects, if any, of our comparisons.

Nevertheless, there have been an enormous number of studies by academic psychologists, often resembling scientific experiments, attempting to get to the truth. While they have sometimes produced conflicting conclusions, the research can still help us understand more about the consequences of our social comparisons.

I have broken down my exploration of the results into several sections, each of which focus on one of the typical targets of our comparisons.

Comparisons through the ages

Siblings

Around 80% of those of us who live in the West have grown up with at least one brother or sister. The fact that we typically spend a huge amount of time with our siblings means they're often the easiest and most obvious candidates for our comparisons, particularly if they're the same sex and of similar age. If we also consider that our brother(s) and sister(s) are generally with us during most of our formative years, it's clear that they hold a uniquely potent position in our lives.

It's not surprising, therefore, that psychologists have studied the impact of sibling relationships for a long time. One of the early theorists was Alfred Adler who, in the first part of the last century, argued that competition and the associated comparisons between siblings were highly influential in the development of children's *personalities*.[1]

He proposed that the first child feels 'dethroned' if a sibling arrives, leading them to try to regain their parents' undivided attention. In so doing, they're often conscientious and seek to dominate their siblings, tending to take leadership roles when older. Middle children are the most likely to feel excluded and often struggle to find their place in the family and, later, in the wider world. Their efforts to fit in, mean that they usually have an 'easy-going' nature. According to Adler, the youngest child is generally the most dependent on others, having been cared for by both parents *and* siblings. This can make them selfish, although they're usually more confident and sociable than their older brothers and sisters.

Adler suggested that as a means of reducing competition and hurtful comparisons, siblings attempt to distinguish themselves from their brothers and sisters by carving out new niches and developing divergent character traits. If, like me, you've ever wondered why siblings are often so completely different from each other this may provide part of the answer.

Much of the initial empirical work testing Adler's birth order theories found support for them. However, recent large-scale quantitative studies have disputed the results, or at least the size of the effects. A 2015 investigation, for example, based on more than 20,000 people living in the US, UK and Germany, found no birth order effects whatsoever on the five main personality traits - extraversion, emotional stability, agreeableness, conscientiousness and imagination.[2] In the same year, a study of nearly 400,000 US high school students uncovered only a tiny association.[3] It's suggested that these investigations were better able to take account of other possible influences on personality, while the fact that average family sizes have fallen significantly since Adler's time, probably helps explain the divergent results as well. The effects are unlikely to be as dramatic where there are fewer siblings.

The more general problem, it seems to me, is that Adler's personality conclusions are too removed from the most likely effects of comparisons to be identifiable. Accurately measuring personality traits is problematic as well. Self-reporting them normally involves answering survey questions to form an aggregate measure of, say, 'agreeableness'. Do you 'cheat to get ahead, use others for your own ends, believe that you are better than others and have good intentions?' are all examples of questions designed to ascertain how agreeable we are. But our answers may vary from one day to the next according to our mood, and, in some instances, will be influenced by who we compare ourselves with to reach a judgement. I also wonder how truthful our responses will be: not everybody who is disagreeable will want to admit this after all!

Many researchers have tried to circumvent these issues by using third parties to assess the personality traits of others. In practice, though, nobody could know a sufficiently large number of individuals - in a statistical sense - well enough to accurately assess their level of 'agreeableness'. Some people will be agreeable when meeting face-to-face, but disagreeable in other situations which the researcher doesn't experience. Alternatively, if a large number of third parties are involved, each with the task of judging a few people, they'll almost certainly have different standards by which they assess them.

With this in mind, it's perhaps no coincidence that the area where the strongest consensus regarding birth order effects exits, is the only area where a truly objective measure is available to test for it – intelligence, as measured by IQ.

Both of the recent research papers I referred to found a relationship between intelligence and birth order, with IQ test scores falling slightly from first to later borns on average. This is thought to reflect the impact of the eldest child (generally) receiving more parental attention than their later born siblings during the first couple of years of life - a crucial period in the development of intelligence. As a younger sibling myself, I hasten to add that the eldest child only has about a 52% chance of having a higher IQ than his/her brother or sister in a two child family!

By implication, children with *no* siblings should presumably also do relatively well in IQ tests once other potential factors, such as genetic influences, are accounted for. Toni Falbo, an expert in the field, looked into this, concluding that only children outperform later borns from *larger* families (those with at least three children), although they typically underperform first borns and those with just one sibling.[4]

While it's hard to pin IQ differences on comparison effects, it's interesting that the large study of US, UK and German individuals I mentioned earlier, found that respondents' *perception* of their intellect also fell in tandem with their birth order position: later borns often *believe* they're not as clever as their older siblings. As we've just discovered, there may be an element of truth in this, but crucially the effect persisted even when taking account of 'actual' intelligence. It seems highly likely that the typical direction of the comparisons made between siblings (upward by the youngest and downward by the eldest) accounts for the result.

The same factor probably explains why studies designed to explore the impact of birth order on overall *self-esteem* have usually unearthed a link as well. The results of a Toni Falbo investigation involving 1,785 undergraduates, for instance, demonstrated that first borns typically have slightly higher self-esteem than last borns.[7] The self-esteem of middle and only children lie somewhere between these extremes, presumably because the former make plenty of upward *and* downward comparisons, while the latter are forced to rely more heavily on lateral comparisons with peers.

The effects may have been even stronger if it wasn't for those instances where younger siblings consistently outperformed their older brother(s) or sister(s), reversing the normal direction of the comparisons and hence the likely effects on self-esteem. Also, as with personality traits, it's not necessarily straightforward to accurately quantify people's self-esteem.

A more helpful framework than Adler's, designed to explicitly assess the impact of comparisons on siblings' psychological well-being, was devised by Abraham Tesser in the late-1980s. His 'Self Evaluation Maintenance Model'[5] suggests that siblings' reactions to comparisons depend largely on three factors:

➤ How they perform relative to their brother or sister in a particular task - do they win or lose?

➤ How (psychologically) close they are to their sibling - is he or she somebody they frequently compare themselves with?

➤ The relevance of the task to their 'self-concept' - does the task matter to them?

Tesser proposed that a child who *underperforms* a sibling they're *close* to - particularly a younger one - on an activity that's *important* to them will experience the most negative effects, feeling worse about themselves as a result of the comparisons they've made. He later incorporated the *possibility* that children can feel better even if they have underperformed, effectively basking in the reflected glory of their sibling, and feel worse if they've outperformed. However, such empathetic reactions are far more likely to be felt when the task doesn't matter much to them but is important to their sibling. They are most commonly reported by identical twins.[6]

Over many years now, the vast majority of experiments designed to test this commonsensical model have yielded supportive results, confirming that siblings (and people more generally) typically respond to the results of their comparisons along the prescribed lines.

As the title of his research suggests, Tesser argued that individuals adopt various strategies to try and minimise the harmful impact of unfavourable comparisons on their self-evaluations. These include spending less time with the target of their comparisons, adopting a hobby different to them or simply blaming bad luck if they have lost or come off worse. The trouble is, there's only a certain number of times we can credibly blame misfortunate for our lack of success, while changing who we compare ourselves with isn't straightforward for the reasons discussed in the previous chapter.

Parents

The behaviour of parents and other caregivers is of course fundamental to children's psychological development, with much of the research in this area designed to uncover the 'holy grail' of parenting - the methods which help yield the most successful, well-balanced offspring. For the record, an 'authoritative' parenting style is typically found to trump both 'authoritarian' and 'permissive' approaches.

My focus is more specific: what happens to those children who, through their comparisons, come to believe that at least one of their caregivers treats them differently to a brother or sister. Given the battle for attention and material possessions it's no surprise to find that siblings are extremely sensitive to comparisons of this sort. The problem is also widespread with between 40% and 80% of children indicating in various surveys that their parents treat them better or worse than a sibling. Parents, of course, have a different view but it's the child's *perception* that matters here.

Judy Dunn was amongst the first to thoroughly investigate the effects of perceived parental favouritism through her pioneering studies of sibling relations within the home. In a 1993 interview with "Psychology Today," she summarised her findings as follows...

'Children are far more socially sophisticated than we ever imagined. That little 15-month or 17-month old is watching like a hawk what goes on between her mother and older sibling. And the greater the difference in the maternal affection and attention, the more hostility and conflict between the siblings.'

This conclusion isn't just important in its own right but also because high levels of sibling 'hostility and conflict' have frequently been linked to bullying, substance abuse and other deviant behaviours both at school and later in life.

Many other investigations have also uncovered a *direct* relationship between different parental treatment and 'poor' conduct in children. Often the results take the form of simple correlations, meaning that we can't be certain that it's the parental favouritism that *causes* the problem behaviour rather than the other way round. But there are plenty of other studies that suggest that this is exactly what happens sometimes.[8]

Patently, a child would require huge resilience *not* to be affected by their parents persistently favouring a sibling or, for that matter, favouring *them* over a sibling. The resulting relatively 'bad' behaviour of one child may then reinforce the favouritism for another, potentially creating a vicious cycle.

Only a handful of studies have examined whether parental favouritism affects children's self-esteem. One such investigation was conducted in 1994 amongst US college students.[9] It found that those who believed there was no favouritism in their family had higher self-esteem than those who thought they were a 'non-favoured' child. Unsurprisingly, the difference was particularly marked when it came to how the students felt about themselves when surrounded by their immediate family - their 'home' self-esteem.

Sibling comparisons of parental treatment are not the only comparisons children make regarding their caregivers. They may also come to compare their abilities to those of their parents. It's often argued that children underperform as a result of unrealistically high (or low) expectations being thrust upon them by their caregivers. But children are also perfectly capable of heaping unreasonable expectations on themselves through comparisons with their parents (or others).

In some ways, this might seem like a perfectly rational thing to do - they're from the same gene pool after all. But such comparisons can be entirely inappropriate for obvious reasons, with problems ensuing for the child as a consequence. There are many high-profile examples of children with 'successful' parents lumping unnecessary pressure on themselves. Equally, the offspring of 'unsuccessful' parents can set their sights far lower than they're capable of achieving. Either way, the outcome is likely to be unsatisfactory.

Partners

Slightly later in life, our partner - the person we share our lives with, whose successes and failures we'll be acutely aware of - is an easy and obvious target of our comparisons. Although we might expect there to be less competition between married or cohabiting couples than occurs in other relationships there's little to suggest that this is true. Even so, it may be that we're less affected by (perceived) differences in our performances or at least better able to suppress their implications for the sake of maintaining harmony.

A study many years ago investigated this issue by examining what happened when 79 married couples competed against each other in a simple game, with the winners and losers being determined randomly.[10] Husbands and wives were found to react as strongly to competition with each other as they did when competing against strangers, while women were more affected than men, particularly to intra-marital competition. It was argued that the latter was consistent with other research suggesting '*Women tend to define themselves in terms of their relationships with their husbands,*' while '*Husbands' careers tend to be the central aspect of their lives.*'

More than 30 years later, have such 'old-fashioned' attitudes changed and the effects with them? A 2017 survey by the Pew Research Centre in the US indicated traditional gender roles appear to remain alive and well. 72% of men and 71% of women agreed that it's '*very important for a man to support his family financially to be a good husband and partner.*' Also, a 2013 University of Chicago study[11] concluded that '*having the wife earn more than the husband increases the likelihood of divorce by 50%.*' When bearing in mind that about a third of women in the West are now paid more than their partners, up from less than 20% in the 1980s, these are perhaps surprising results.

Dig a little deeper and things become even more interesting. The same Chicago study discovered that when a woman out earns her spouse the risk of divorce was only higher among more educated couples – defined as those that had gone to university. Meanwhile, a 2016 investigation, also in the US, concluded that in instances where the woman earned more than her male partner, the divorce risk was greater among those couples that married in the late-1960s and 1970s than those that wed in the 1990s.[12] The improvement among more recently married couples, however, entirely reflected relationships where the husband was 'middle-earning' or didn't have a degree. University educated partners were still more likely to divorce when the wife was the main bread winner, supporting the results of the Chicago report.

It's not clear why the level of education should be so critical, although a couple of theories have been advanced. The last 20 years has seen those with relatively few years of formal education bear the brunt of the widespread income squeeze, meaning that a relationship involving two such people has effectively *forced* them both to work. This in turn, the argument runs, has made it increasingly normal and acceptable for a wife to enjoy higher pay than her husband. In contrast, partners who have received university education may still be in a position to *choose* whether they both work, suggesting that traditional gender roles are more likely to apply.

Peers

Peer comparisons are especially rife in education and work as well as during parenthood.

- Parenthood

The last of these may surprise some, but those with children will know how endemic they are at this stage of life. Not only do the vast majority of us actively compare our parenting abilities with fellow parents but we're acutely aware of how our child(ren) are performing relative to their peers. This tends to be particularly true of the first child where we have no previous experience to fall back on.

Often these comparisons are extremely valuable. If, for example, we discover that our child is *significantly* behind others of the same age in reaching key stages of development it may point to problems that are better dealt with sooner rather than later. Also, if our comparisons lead us to conclude that we're considerably stricter or more lenient than our fellow parents this could sensibly lead us to reassess our parenting style.

Nevertheless, as with all comparisons, there are plenty of things that can go wrong. Given how important our children are, it's very easy to make too many comparisons and worry overly about their outcomes. The comparisons themselves may also be unreasonable, such as comparing our perfectly able son or daughter with a child who is particularly gifted or one experiencing learning difficulties for instance. We might envy peers who appear to have exceptionally well-behaved children, possibly learning the wrong lessons about the 'correct' way to parent.

While this area is hugely under-researched, there's no doubt that any of these situations can have profound consequences. In the last section we saw how parental favouritism creates behavioural and psychological problems in siblings and the same must logically apply to children whose caregiver(s) persistently tell them how badly or fantastically they're performing relative to their peers. Inappropriate comparisons may also affect the mental health of the parents themselves, making them feel as though they have 'failed', while disagreements over child rearing techniques sometimes lead to relationship difficulties. Marriage counsellors have estimated that parenting disputes contribute to about 20% of divorces in the West.

- School

There's an unusually strong consensus within the research community concerning the direction of the comparisons made by children in school and the effects they have. After reviewing more than a hundred relevant studies, five academics summarised the situation as follows...

'..pupils prefer to compare their performances upward - specifically with pupils who are better than themselves but who resemble themselves on related and unrelated attributes....Such upward comparisons not only lead pupils to perform better but evoke negative affect and lower academic self-concept.'[13]

Put another way, most students want to improve and attempt to do so by looking to those who have similar characteristics but are marginally 'superior' to them in important respects. The evidence strongly indicates that the comparisons work - children generally do improve academically by comparing upward. But there's a catch. The upward comparisons also lead students to feel worse about themselves, particularly - and ironically - with regard to their academic abilities.

An important word in the quote above is 'prefer'. The obvious question is what happens if the ideal target for academic comparisons simply doesn't exist or is too time-consuming to find? We know that children gravitate towards students of the same sex, age, religion and/or socioeconomic status - probably meaning that they compare themselves with one or two close friends. *If* those friends are not as talented as they are and hence downward comparisons are typical, then academic performance has been shown to suffer in certain circumstances.[14]

In truth, not all studies have concluded that upward comparisons yield negative psychological outcomes. It's been found that children can avoid harmful self-evaluations when they compare upwards specifically for the purpose of self-improvement. This is an issue I will return to later on when considering the benefits upward comparisons can bring.

Some pupils are also more vulnerable to the adverse side-effects of upward comparisons than others: in particular those who believe that they're at the bottom of the class as well as 'older' students. The former are likely to make a greater number of upward comparisons than most and the latter more in the way of self-evaluative ones. The nature of children's comparisons has been shown to change as they advance through school. Initially pupils are mainly concerned with comparisons that help them understand how to behave and complete tasks. It's only later - from around the age of seven - that they begin to use comparisons to tell them how they're performing relative to their classmates.

Academic comparisons are obviously not the only ones children and adolescents make while in education. They also compare their home life with peers, which, when they are facing difficulties, will often bring a yearning for 'normality'. Comparisons involving physical appearance, sporting abilities, hobbies and other interests feature regularly as well. I will consider the influence of some of these in the next chapter which focusses on the influence of social media.

- Work

Several years ago, an ex-boss of mine returned from a client meeting to be asked by a colleague how his presentation went. His memorable response was '*Do you know what, it was one of those meetings where you come out feeling like you're the master of the universe.*' There was no doubt he meant it as well!

This is an extreme illustration of what can happen if somebody makes a lot of downward comparisons and are frequently informed that they're very good at their job. But the research on social comparisons in the workplace suggests that 'contrast' effects - feeling better about ourselves following downward comparisons and worse after upward ones - are dominant in competitive environments.

One such study involved nearly 1,000 alumni from a large Canadian university who were employed in a wide range of occupations.[15] It discovered that those who made more downward comparisons enjoyed greater job satisfaction, were more committed to their employer and less inclined to look for a new job. Correspondingly, workers who predominantly made upward comparisons were usually less satisfied, less committed and more active in seeking alternative employment. The study suggested that having an ambiguous role, low task autonomy and a low opinion of yourself were good predictors of upward comparisons.

Only in working environments where competition is low and empathy high have, to my knowledge, assimilation effects - a feeling of closeness in a psychological sense to others - been found to dominate. A study of healthcare workers, for example, showed that they tended to identify with those colleagues worse-off than themselves, rather than feeling better as a result of their downward comparisons.

Another fascinating study of the effects of workplace comparisons examined how employees responded to wage cuts.[16] Workers were placed in teams of two, completed the same individual tasks and, initially, received the same wage irrespective of their productivity. The researchers discovered that cutting the pay of both workers by the same amount caused performance to deteriorate sharply. More interestingly, however, when the wage of just one of the workers was reduced, that person's output declined *more than twice as much as the performance decrease when both workers' wages were cut.'*

The conclusion is clear - it really matters to us how we're rewarded *relative* to the target of our comparisons: the demotivating influence of a wage reduction is far bigger if our immediate colleague is not experiencing the same thing. This effect doesn't just apply to pay either. In virtually any circumstance, the perception that we're being treated badly in an absolute sense is one thing but the feeling that we're being treated badly *and* unfairly compared to somebody else is quite another.

The comparisons we make with work colleagues and other peers (as well as our past-selves) are also largely responsible for so-called 'midlife crises' – defined by "MedicineNet" as a *'period of personal emotional turmoil and coping challenges that some people encounter when they reach middle age, accompanied by a desire for change in their lives brought on by fears and anxieties about growing older.'* We might think, for example, 'I'm 55 and have achieved so little compared with everybody else,' 'I look so much older than my work colleagues' or 'My best days are behind me now.' Such thoughts lead us to feel worse about ourselves with potentially meaningful consequences for our mental health.

There's a vigorous debate within the academic community whether such crises exist, although it seems to me that this mainly reflects a squabble about the technicalities of the label itself, rather than anything more meaningful. There can be no doubt that age-related insecurities of the sort I have described are very real, particularly for those of us living in cultures that value youthfulness over experience. Midlife crises are far less apparent in the East where, in general, age and wisdom are more highly prized assets.

Empirical evidence for the existence of midlife crises may be provided by the UK Office for National Statistics' (ONS') annual well-being survey. Covering roughly 150,000 people aged between 16 and 90, it asks a number of questions including 'To what extent do you feel the things you do in your life are worthwhile?' 'How satisfied are you with your life nowadays?' and 'How happy did you feel yesterday?' Intriguingly, the aggregate scores on each of these questions are always lower among 40-54 year-olds than they are in the immediately older and younger age groups. The standard explanation is that our own needs are being sandwiched between those of our children and our aging parents during this period in our lives. But I suspect the impact of many of the comparisons we make at this 'midlife' stage are playing a role as well.

- Retirement

The same ONS survey reveals that 60-79 year-olds generally enjoy the *highest* self-worth of any age group. Again, several factors may be at play here but I would venture that our relative lack of harmful comparisons during retirement helps explain the result. I have argued that we're particularly prone to making comparisons at school, work and when we have young children. By the time we're 60+ most of us will be through these life stages and, even if we're still working, the extent of our ambition could have dimmed somewhat. Sadly, the size of our peer group may also diminish.

In brief

Though the people we compare ourselves with may change as we get older, the fact that our comparisons have significant effects on our thoughts and deeds does not. That much is clear from the academic research. It's also evident that the frequency of our comparisons and the nature of their effects will vary depending on who we are, what we do and how we perceive ourselves to be placed relative to those we compare ourselves with.

Persistent upward comparisons have consistently been found to have detrimental effects on our psychological well-being, including our self-esteem, while downward comparisons generally give us a psychological boost. There are some exceptions to this, although they are few and far between.

Chapter 3

The Role of Social Media

The advent of social media, including platforms such as Facebook, YouTube, Instagram, Snapchat and Twitter, has provided a hugely powerful means to access information about countless people as well as providing the opportunity to interact directly with a previously unimaginable number of individuals. The figures below illustrate the extraordinary reach and potential influence social media already has.

➢ The global number of social media users in 2018 was 3.2 billion, representing 42% of the world's population (Smart Insights).

➢ There were 44 million active social media users in the UK alone in January 2018 and well over 200 million in the US (Statista).

➢ The average user spends nearly 2 hours a day on social media. It's much higher for teenagers (mediakix, 2018).

➢ 28% of young people in the UK 'constantly' use social media, 18% 'several times an hour' and 29% 'several times a day' (2017 Annual Bullying Survey).

➢ 10% of teens check their phones more than ten times *per night* (mediakix, 2018).

Spot the difference

As we discovered in the last two chapters, where there's social interaction there will be comparisons and where there are comparisons there will be effects on our psychological well-being. Of course, if the comparisons we now make via social media have simply replaced those we used to make through face-to-face interactions, the net impact could in theory be zero. But there are several reasons to believe that neither the nature nor the number of comparisons are the same.

First, social media sites allow us to carefully tailor the image we present of ourselves to the outside world in a way that's impossible with in-person contact. When we have total control over what content to show, not only are we likely to be 'economical with the truth', only posting material that presents ourselves in a positive light, but we may lose contact with the truth itself - doctoring images for example. Some are even prepared to undergo cosmetic surgery to improve their appearance, with many plastic surgeons reporting that, *'looking better in selfies'* is a frequently mentioned motivation for a procedure.

These practices mean that we're likely to make far more upward comparisons than we otherwise would, comparing our *true* offline selves with *biased* online versions of others. Even if we're providing misleading information about ourselves it's still strangely easy to believe that those we're comparing ourselves with are somehow better placed than us.

Second, social media sites offer unique insights into people's social network. We can easily discover exactly how many 'Followers,' 'Friends,' 'Reacts,' 'Likes,' 'Retweets,' 'Views' and 'Snapstreaks' others have, potentially drawing influential conclusions about our (relative) popularity from this information.

Third, many of the inhibitions we feel when communicating with somebody face-to-face melt away when we're a safe distance apart, tapping out messages on a keyboard. Different, usually undesirable, character traits often rise to the surface in these circumstances, just as they can when we're behind the wheel of a car. Sadly, as with road-rage, online-message-rage occurs far too frequently.

Fourth, social media provides the possibility of making comparisons with a virtually unlimited number of people at any time of our choosing. This obviously isn't so easily accomplished with face-to-face or indeed any other form of social interaction.

The effects

By far the biggest study to investigate the link between people's psychological well-being and the rise of social media (as well as other forms of electronic communication) involved 1.1 million American adolescents.[1] The report, published in 2018, tapped into the nationally representative annual survey of US eighth, tenth and twelfth graders which, among many things, records teenagers' self-esteem, life satisfaction and happiness, together with the time they spend on various on and off-screen activities.

Having improved through much of the previous 30 years, the authors noted that measures of mental health amongst 13-18 year-olds suddenly deteriorated after 2012, roughly coinciding with the widespread adoption of smartphones and associated use of social media: ownership of smartphones by teens increased from 37% in 2012 to 89% in 2018. While a simple correlation of this sort hardly represents proof that the increase in screen time *caused* the decline in well-being, the authors made several additional observations which, when taken together, strengthen the case.

➢ Eighth and tenth graders who engaged with social media for at least 40 hours a week were around twice as likely to describe themselves as 'unhappy' relative to those using it only a few hours a week.

➢ Compared with those who used social media 1-2 hours a week, eighth and tenth graders who spent 10-19 hours a week on it were more than 40% likely to be unhappy.

➢ The least happy adolescents were those with low in-person social interaction and high usage of electronic communication. The opposite was true of the happiest individuals.

➢ Psychological well-being was lower in years when adolescents spent more time on screens and higher in years when they spent less time on them.

➢ The increase in social media activity slightly *preceded* the fall in psychological well-being rather than the other way around.

➢ Other, frequently mentioned, causes of the deterioration in mental health, such as unemployment and time spent on homework, had little or no correlation with well-being.

The paper concluded that the declining mental health of US teenagers was...

'...*possibly due to their spending more time on electronic communication and less time on non-screen activities such as in-person social interaction. The rapid adoption of smartphone technology in the early 2010s may have had a marked negative impact on adolescents' psychological well-being.'*

There's no shortage of anecdotal support for this argument as indicated by the following quotes...

- *'With social media it sort of forces you to try and meet a standard and if you're below it you start to feel a bit low about yourself'* (Girl, aged 14: Sky News story 19.9.18).

- *'I see all my friends having a good time on social media and it gets me down. I feel like no one cares enough to invite me'* (Teenage boy talking to ChildLine: BBC News story, 3.7.18).

- Social media *'has increased my level of anxiety and social anxiety...I'm constantly worried what others think of my posts and pictures.'* (20-24 year old: Quoted in 2017 Royal Society for Public Health, Status of Mind Report).

- *'Social interaction...I think we've lost due to always being on our phones, always thinking that we have to show everybody else what we're up to and in reality life isn't always happy. We do get down. We need to take a break and step away from this fake illusion of happiness 24-7 and enjoying ourselves all the time.'* (Woman, aged 18: Radio 5 Live 26.9.18).

- *'I've been struggling...and I think social media can sometimes really not help with that...You see people saying what they're up to and what they're doing and their house always seems lovely and tidy and the kids seem well-behaved, and they always look nice and slim...There are lots of reasons - you compare yourself to them.'* (Jason Manford, the comedian: Sky News story, 8.5.19).

- *'Teens can have thousands of friends online and yet feel unsupported and isolated...Technology - including social media - could be exacerbating social isolation'* (Cal Strode from Mental Health Foundation, reacting to a survey showing that almost 10% of people aged 16-24 were 'always' or 'often' lonely: BBC News story 3.7.18).

- *'Are we all too busy to make space and time for our children? Or is it the illusion created by social networks that everyone else is liked, popular and enjoying a far more exciting life so they feel lonelier than ever'* (Esther Rantzen, founder of ChildLine: BBC News story 3.7.18).

Before rushing to condemn all social media as unequivocally bad for our mental health, however, we need to explore several issues further.

Does exposure to social media *cause* poor mental health?

One study has shown that individuals with low self-esteem often see social media as a relatively safe and appealing forum in which to express themselves,[2] implying that the apparent link between mental health and social media use may work in the opposite direction to that suggested in the US report. It's also conceivable that the relationship operates in *both* directions - poor well-being leading to greater social media activity and greater social media activity leading to poor well-being. Support for this was provided by the same study which found that people generally responded unhelpfully to comments posted by those seeking reassurance, making their situation worse.

Nevertheless, there are now many studies that have convincingly demonstrated a direct, adverse social media effect on people's psychological well-being. A week-long experiment involving nearly 1,100 participants in Denmark, for example, concluded that taking a break from Facebook had favourable effects on 'life satisfaction' and led to more positive emotions generally.[3] Similarly, a US study showed Facebook use *predicted* declines in well-being amongst 82 people with an average age of 20, while the same was *not* true of 'direct social interaction'.[4] Also, the more time people spent on Facebook, the bigger was the reduction in their well-being.

A 2018 investigation of students aged 18-22 by researchers at the University of Pennsylvania uncovered a causal link as well.[5] 143 participants were randomly assigned to two groups - a control group that maintained their typical social media behaviour and an experimental one whose time on Facebook, Snapchat and Instagram was restricted to 10 minutes per platform per day for three weeks. The second group reported sizeable improvements in both 'depression' and 'loneliness' at the end of the period, with the largest increases coming among those who had the worst depression scores to begin with.

How are contradictory studies and anecdotal evidence of positive effects explained?

There's no doubt that social media has improved social connectivity enormously. And this in turn must have yielded some benefits, even *if* it has come at the cost of reduced face-to-face interaction. So what explains the fact that only a handful of studies have uncovered positive (or even negligible) effects?

Part of the answer may be provided by a large UK study in 2016 which found that while *moderate* use of technology can be advantageous, the negative effects overwhelm the positives after a certain point.[6] That point varies a little depending on the particular electronic activity involved, but is generally about an hour a day according to the research. Until that juncture, 'mental well-being' was found to rise, before falling progressively thereafter. In the case of smartphones (the study did not explicitly investigate social media activity), well-being had dropped below its starting point after 2-3 hours of daily use.

The huge investigation of US adolescents I referred to earlier, came to the same conclusion when testing directly for the effects of social media on 'happiness'. It also found that the negative effects of social media were much bigger for eighth and tenth graders than they were for twelfth graders. This could provide a clue to another part of the answer. If, as is often the case, academic studies investigate the reactions of 'young people' to social media activity then adverse consequences are more likely to be detected than if the responses of older students or adults are scrutinised.

Why do we continue using social media if the effects are apparently so damaging?

The answer to this conundrum almost certainly lies with the addictive or, at the very least, the habit-forming nature of social media. In a Sky News story in September 2018, Dr. Richard Graham, consultant psychiatrist at the Nightingale Hospital in London, was quoted as saying...

'We think social media affects dopamine levels through the different rewards they offer...In the forms of likes or increased followers or retweets, or whatever platform it is, it gives you a little bit of a lift in your mood...What's key to addiction is some sort of mood modification where you might get a buzz and then of course you want more.'

In the same story, an app designer likened the pull down action necessary to refresh many social media feeds to that of a slot machine. She also noted the heavy use of the colour red in many notifications, suggesting that the *'human eye loves red'* as it's both warm and indicates urgency.

A review of the empirical research on the subject of social media addiction, published in 2017, argued that the Fear Of Missing Out (FOMO) and the associated Nomophobia (no mobile phone phobia) helps explain the issue as well.[7]

'There appears to be an inherent understanding or requirement in today's technology-loving culture that one needs to engage in online social networking in order not to miss out, to stay up to date, and to connect.'

The report pointed to a number of studies that show FOMO is linked to lower self-esteem, heightened anxiety and symptoms of depression in heavy users of social networking sites.

It's hard to be precise about the extent of social media addiction, although most studies suggest that it's not as virulent as we might imagine it to be in the West at least (several Chinese studies have found it be higher there). For instance, the results of a 2015 survey of young teenagers in the Netherlands[8] showed that only about 5% could be classified as addicted.

But I suspect this reflects a definitional issue more than anything else. Interestingly, the Ipsos Q3 2018 Tech Tracker survey of roughly 1,000 British people, found 78% of 18-24 year olds agreeing that they spend *'too much time looking at their phones.'* Given that 72% of this age group visit social network sites on their devices, more than any other phone related activity, it's safe to say that a majority of teenagers effectively acknowledge that they have an issue with social media usage. Backing this up, a 2017 survey by "Ditch The Label," an anti-bullying charity, found 61% of young people in the UK agreeing that they *'couldn't go more than a day'* without checking social media.

When the Royal Society for Public Health (RSPH) launched "Scroll Free September" in 2018, it cited the results of a survey showing that 33% of all social media users and 47% of 'young' users (aged 18-34) thought that if they quit for a month this would have a positive effect on their *'overall mental health and well-being'*. 40% of young users believed that it would improve their *'body confidence and self-esteem'*. These results again imply an addiction issue.

The same organisation published the findings of another survey, taken among 14-24 year olds in the UK, as part of its 2017 #StatusofMind report. It revealed that the net impact on health and well-being of Twitter, Facebook, Snapchat and Instagram were all considered to be negative by the users themselves! Only YouTube was thought to be of (modest) net benefit. While the platforms were generally accepted to promote 'self-expression' and 'self-identity', FOMO, together with sleep deprivation and bullying, were some of the primary negatives.

Are *social comparisons* to blame for the negative effects?

So far I have only hinted at the role social comparisons play in explaining the detrimental effects of intense social media activity. But the little research that has been conducted in this area to date suggests that they are indeed highly influential.

A US study of undergraduate students at Utah State University,[9] for example, discovered that those spending a relatively large amount of time on Facebook were more likely to agree that other users were *'happier and had better lives than themselves'*. Another paper discovered that college-age students who compared themselves unfavourably with others on social networking sites put themselves at risk of 'rumination' and, as a consequence, symptoms of depression.[10]

The most thorough investigation of relevance involved 145 undergraduates from a Midwestern university in the US.[11] It revealed that the more they looked at Facebook the more, mainly upward, social comparisons they made on the site.

Upward comparisons via the platform were found to be associated with lower self-esteem. Given these results were derived purely from simple correlation analysis, the authors also adopted an experimental approach to examine whether temporary exposure to upward and downward social media comparisons *caused* self-evaluation and self-esteem to be affected. Sure enough, the participants in the experiment reported lower self-esteem having looked at a fictional person's high activity social network compared to a low activity one. The student's self-evaluation was also negatively impacted by upward comparisons, while downward comparisons had no obvious effect.

A handful of research papers have investigated the relationship between Facebook activity and body dissatisfaction amongst women, typically finding a positive correlation between the two – the greater the usage the higher the dissatisfaction. As before, however, it's important to stress that this doesn't prove causality.

A more detailed UK experiment, involving 112 female students and staff aged 17-25, suggested that there was *no* evidence that exposure to Facebook led young women to feel unhappier about their bodies.[12] However, it did put them in a more negative mood, while '*For women who make more appearance comparisons, spending time on Facebook led to greater desire to change their face, hair and skin-related features.*' The authors argued that by shifting the emphasis to 'selfies' and away from full-body images, social networking sites had effectively encouraged far more facial comparisons.

Another important difference between social networking sites and more traditional varieties of media is that the former involve a greater number of comparisons with *peers* as opposed to ultra-thin models and celebrities. We might think this would be less hurtful although the bulk of evidence indicates that the effects are surprisingly similar.[13]

Social comparisons via the various platforms also contribute to 'cyber-bullying' as some use them to exploit their relatively powerful position, putting others down to feel better about themselves. Although the reported incidence of such bullying differs between surveys, the most shocking numbers were reported in the #StatusofMind study I mentioned. It suggests that a staggering 70% of young people have experienced it at some point, with 37% suffering regularly. According to the Royal Society for Public Health, '*Victims of bullying are more likely to experience low academic performance, depression, anxiety, self-harm, feelings of loneliness and changes in eating and sleeping patterns.*'

Based on a 2016 survey of 2745 UK secondary school pupils aged 11-16, University of Warwick research concluded that 'cyber-victimisation' had similar adverse effects on behaviour and self-esteem as more traditional types of bullying.[14] It also discovered that cyber-bullying doesn't create many *new* victims - those affected were almost always subject to more traditional forms of bullying already. Although good news in one sense, it's very bad news for the victims themselves who are now hounded around the clock. Not surprisingly, these students were found to have the lowest self-esteem of all participants.

In brief

Social networking sites have dramatically changed both the nature and frequency of our comparisons. Importantly, we're more likely to make upward comparisons as we flick through the images and text others *choose* to make available of themselves, comparing them with unbiased versions of ourselves.

Work assessing the effects of social media activity on our mental health is still in its infancy although there is a growing consensus that they are generally harmful, at least for the many young people using the various platforms for more than 2-3 hours a day. Our self-esteem has been shown to suffer as a result of heavy usage and benefit from abstinence. Nevertheless, most of us still can't put our smartphones down and our keyboards away partly for Fear Of Missing Out. The use of social media has become a habit, verging on an addiction, for countless numbers of people across the world. Only now, however, are the providers beginning to address the downsides of their earth-shattering, comparison-generating inventions.

Chapter 4

Spotting the Signs, Understanding the Triggers

I have argued that our social comparisons are often misleading and it's very easy to react inappropriately to them. This is generally a consequence of circumstance rather than our own or anybody else's fault. I have also explored numerous academic studies of their effects, most of which indicate that they can have powerful implications for our psychological well-being. Meanwhile, social networking sites have provided a hugely important new forum for comparisons, with the weight of evidence suggesting that their *intensive* use also creates problems, particularly for teenagers.

Of course, not all mental health issues are attributable to unhelpful comparisons. So how can we be confident that the issues we face are the result of the comparisons we (or others) have made? In many cases, we'll know only too well but often we won't, either because the relevant comparisons have been lost in the mists of time or they have become so habitual that we don't even realise that we're making them. Below are what I consider to be the most common telltale signs, both in the way we think and how we behave.

Thought signals

➤ We believe that everybody is better than us. This might relate to one particular aspect of our lives or everything about us. We may convince ourselves that we're 'utterly useless' and not worth knowing.

➤ We think that we have to be the best at everything we do. Our self-worth is critically dependent on proving to ourselves and others that we're better than the rest.

➤ We're extremely envious of other peoples' physical characteristics or abilities that we prize personally. We put them on a pedestal and think of ways to be more like them.

➤ We spend a lot of time worrying about what other people are thinking about us, implicitly assuming that they're making hurtful comparisons and disapproving of us in some way. There's often nothing to suggest that this is the case.

➤ We find it very hard to enjoy our successes, writing them off as meaningless achievements or feeling that we should have done even better than we did.

➤ We can't enjoy the success of others, not least those of close family and friends. We think of their success as our comparative failure; what they've achieved, we haven't.

➤ We experience the precise opposite of the first point, believing that we're far superior to everybody else. This is most likely to reflect a form of personal defence mechanism but can also reflect genuine arrogance.

Behavioural signals

➢ We withdraw quickly from many activities or avoid them altogether for fear of being worse than others. This includes social situations, particular tasks and/or new opportunities.

➢ We much prefer spending time with people of very different ages or backgrounds to ourselves. This minimises the chances of hurtful comparisons.

➢ We're ultra-competitive even in the most minor of competitions, playing to win at all costs and often cheating to do so. We react extremely badly to defeat.

➢ We try too hard to make an impression, often interrupting, freezing or appearing stilted in the company of others.

➢ Our mood and behaviour is highly dependent on what others say or do. It can swing violently between elation and despair in reaction to the most minor of remarks or other perceived slights and praise that involve comparisons either directly or indirectly. We constantly seek approval and are desperate to please.

➢ We're always trying to 'score points' in conversation, often putting others down verbally, or even physically, to strengthen our case. Arguments can stem from the most innocuous of comments.

➢ We're defensive or aggressive when dealing with authority figures. We see them as enemies which threaten us in some way.

> ➢ We're reluctant to listen and respond positively to other people's points of view, believing that we know best and are always right.

I would wager that everybody reading this book will have thought or behaved in ways that resemble at least one of the descriptions mentioned. My focus is on those of us who *persistently* experience many of these symptoms and feel that their lives are being seriously affected as a result. If, like me, you're one of those people, it's time to take action. If you're not, then you may know somebody who is and will want to understand more about what is happening.

Comparisons, schemas and mental health

The first thing to recognise is that people are not necessarily coming up to us and pointing out our relative inadequacies. Instead, we've become conditioned to think about ourselves in an unhelpful way as a result of previous or ongoing comparisons. Whether we're aware of it or not, *we* are usually the ones telling *ourselves* that we're inadequate or incredible. After all, this is consistent with the picture we have of ourselves and, as everybody knows, pictures never lie!

These images, known as schemas in the language of psychology, are usually activated automatically by internal thoughts and/or external prompts. For example, our boss may ask us to deliver a presentation to a large audience, triggering our public speaking schema. We perceive ourselves to have done much worse than colleagues in the past and conclude, 'I'm bound to fail again and make a fool of myself in the process. My reputation will be destroyed.'

With these thoughts occupying our mind, we waste precious time considering how to get out of the talk, rather than what we can do to make it as interesting and informative as possible. If, having given the presentation, we believe that we've performed poorly our public speaking schema will be supplemented by the negative images and thoughts associated with the experience. Our internal beliefs may now be so firmly set that if we're persuaded to present again and receive positive feedback we don't believe it. We conclude either that people are 'just being nice' or it was a one-off.

On another occasion, we're invited to a party. Based on experience we *know* that we won't enjoy it or, worse still, it will upset us. 'Every time I go to something like this all the other guests have interesting and amusing things to say. I'm so boring in comparison. I haven't done anything exciting and I don't have any funny stories to tell.' If we do attend, we feel tense and, even if it proves to be better than expected, we'll probably still endure the same thought processes next time.

At this stage, I should note that it's perfectly possible, if not likely, to feel inferior in some circumstances and superior in others. This happens when our comparisons have led us to adopt contrasting schemas for different situations. Having done much better than our classmates in a previous music test, for example, we may approach future such exams with confidence - 'I'm good at music and I'm certain I'll do brilliantly again.' Meanwhile, we might have compared our mathematical abilities with our elder brother and determined that, 'I'm terrible at maths and don't have a chance of passing the arithmetic test next week.'

By continually accessing one negative schema or having many different harmful schemas that are triggered frequently it's not hard to see how our mental health can deteriorate. In some cases, we might as well have somebody standing next to us, shouting hurtful things in our ear for the majority of the day; the potential effects, such as those I've mentioned, are likely to be the same. In extreme cases, severe anxiety disorders and depression will be the ultimate result.

Sky News ran a troubling story in May 2018, highlighting the travails of those living with Body Dysmorphic Disorder (BDD).

Sufferers become obsessed with their physical imperfections, which, in many cases, are purely imaginary. They'll go to any length to cover the perceived flaw(s) and may not be able to leave home without a panic attack ensuing. One of them wrote...

'At its worst, I would think about my appearance and how ugly I was for most of the day. I would refuse to attend school and would make excuses so I didn't have to socialise with friends. My makeup would take about three hours and if I did end up going out I would check myself in reflective mirrors and shop windows...People have said that I am really pale and I have goofy teeth. I feel like I am always trying to get people's approval as well as my own...Looking back I realise the negative effect social media has had on my illness. I would compare myself to unrealistic photo-shopped models.'

Labour MP, Chris Evans, had similar issues when younger, comparing himself with film stars Arnold Schwarzenegger and Sylvester Stallone whom, he believed, *'had everything worked out.'* After several hours of training each day Mr. Evans said...

'I'd check myself out in the mirror - if I wasn't happy with what I was doing, I would constantly just pick one exercise, for example bicep curls, and constantly do them until I was fatigued.'

Meanwhile, Adam Collard, a contestant on reality TV show "Love Island," explained his experience of BDD as follows...

'I found myself constantly comparing (myself) to everybody else and because I was unhappy at the time with how I actually looked, I think that's where it all began,' adding that, *'the pressure (to achieve certain physiques) is growing and is even worse in males right now.'*

The importance of perception

One of the key messages to come from these quotes is that we don't have to be 'inferior' to be utterly convinced that we are. This is something a lot of people find very difficult to understand. But, as we've seen, it's our perception that matters and that perception can be completely divorced from any 'normal' sense of reality if inappropriate comparisons have repeatedly been made.

The point is further illustrated by the fact that so many 'successful' people simply don't accept they're successful, experiencing the same damaging thoughts, behaving in the same destructive ways and encountering the same mental health problems that I've set out in this chapter. Take Andre Agassi, an eight-time Grand Slam tennis champion and Olympic gold medalist, for instance. Talking to Jenn Horton from Oprah.com in December 2009, he explained...

'A lot of times I felt like I was craving not losing. The pain of losing was always worse than the joy of winning for me. Winning felt meaningless; it felt like I had dodged a bullet for the day. Losing made me feel less about myself. That's why many times you could always see so much fear in my eyes...Internally, I'm playing scared and in fear of losing...Then I got to the final of the US Open. I'm 26-0, I lose to Pete (Sampras). I kind of conclude you can win 26 matches, lose one and still feel like a loser. It just heightens the point of pointlessness...I didn't like tennis, and I liked myself even less.'

As 'success' is such an imprecise term, one person's definition of it can be very different from another's. It is itself a relative concept, meaning that somebody, whom the vast majority of us would consider successful, can feel like a failure if they compare themselves with an individual they deem to be better. 'My Dad says I'm good at speaking French but I'm not as fluent as Alice, while Tom can speak both French and Spanish brilliantly. I must be really bad at languages.' Or 'I know I earn £40,000 a year, but my colleague Steve is paid £50,000 and my neighbour has told me he gets £60,000 most years. I should be doing much better than I am.'

In brief

Signs of a comparison related disorder involve persistent and troubling thoughts of inferiority, superiority or both. Our harmful thinking will generally manifest itself in submissive, aggressive and/or dominant moods and behaviours as well. The chances are that we'll spend a lot of time feeling useless or, at the other extreme, like 'masters of the universe'.

The reasons for our thoughts, moods and actions are not always obvious and can be triggered by real or imaginary situations. To the extent that we're able to verbalise our thoughts, they may seem completely irrational to others. Everybody can tell us that we're good at something and yet we'll still be certain that we're not. Unfortunately, it's all too easy for our comparison inspired problems to lead to serious mental health issues that need to be addressed.

Chapter 5

The 'Target-Self'

Before contemplating how we can improve our situation, it's essential to establish what it is we're looking to achieve. In particular, what sort of social comparisons will our Target-Selves *choose* to make and how will our Target-Selves react to those comparisons?

Without targets it's very easy to get distracted, confused or deterred as we try to progress. Also, once our conscious mind is geared towards achieving a clear objective, our subconscious has a helpful knack of getting to work as well. It's why we sometimes wake up in the morning with the answer to a question we've been pondering without success the day before.

Three objectives...

Based on what we've learnt about comparisons and their effects, we should keep the following objectives firmly in mind...

1. To be resilient to upward comparisons that will represent a genuine source of motivation and learning

Currently, we're 'damaged' by most upward comparisons as the perception that somebody is better than us automatically makes us believe that we're inferior to them. Often, we don't just feel that we're a lesser person than the individual we're comparing ourselves with but more generally as well. As such, these comparisons serve no positive purpose whatsoever, simply filling our mind with hurtful thoughts.

Our Target-Selves think in a completely different way. Upward comparisons don't undermine our sense of self-worth but are deemed genuinely useful, representing a handy means to motivate and improve. We even actively seek out those more expert than ourselves as a source of learning. The targets of our upward comparisons can be younger or older; more experienced or less experienced; smarter or not as smart; wealthier or poorer than us. These are no longer the criteria we use to determine whether, or who, to ask for help. The only thing that matters is that the person may have insights that we currently lack. Being intimidated by others is a thing of the past.

2. To no longer rely on downward comparisons to inflate our ego

Downward comparisons can represent a quick and easy way to feel better about ourselves. Consciously or not, some of us use them for exactly this purpose and bolster our self-esteem as a result. But we need to be careful here. Frequently putting others down to feel better about ourselves is to live a blinkered, negative life, akin to that of a bully, without (hopefully) the use of their physical or verbal intimidation tactics.

There's another issue to be aware of as well. A 2006 research paper examined the relationship between the self-esteem of a random selection of more than 60 adults and their experience of 'destructive' emotions and behaviours.[1] It concluded that an individual's level of self-esteem was *unable* to predict things like envy, defensiveness, blame and lying. Put another way, we can have a relatively high level of self-esteem - by always comparing downwards for example - and yet still experience a wide range of adverse traits. The study discovered that the people most likely to experience these damaging behaviours and emotions were precisely those who compared themselves frequently with others.

A much better way of living is to have a sufficient, *genuine* sense of security and self-confidence not to require the use of downward comparisons to boost our ego. We'll still make downward comparisons but mainly to generate empathy for others and to track our progress (see below).

3. *To make comparisons with our past and Target-Selves purely to monitor progress and remind ourselves of where we're heading*

In working towards our goals we'll inevitably endure some bad moments and difficult days. It's at these times that making downward comparisons with our past-selves to remind us of the progress we've made is particularly important.

We'll also make upward comparisons with our Target-Selves. They will help us keep our objectives in mind, nudging us towards them and not letting us forget why we're doing what we're doing. When using these comparisons, we'll remember our second objective, not allowing them to undermine our mental well-being but deploying them to inspire and motivate.

Making comparisons of this sort will help us become the 'best we can' - a cliché, but a far healthier, more constructive goal than striving to be better than everybody else. It's importance is recognised by many high-achievers. Having retired from the English cricket team in September 2018, Alistair Cook, the country's leading run-scorer of all time in Test matches and ex captain of the side, pointed out...

'The one thing I can be proud of...I genuinely believe I've become the best player I could have become. You can't compare yourself to anyone else.'

...for a stronger, healthier, happier you

If we can move towards these objectives then the problems I set out at the beginning of the last chapter will start to be replaced by thoughts and behaviours that are far more positive. Ultimately...

➢ We'll be aware of our strengths and weaknesses but not boastful about the former or worried by the latter.

➢ We won't be threatened by competitive environments, enjoying our successes as well as those of people we care for.

➢ We'll see losses and failures as potential learning experiences not triggers for mental self-harm.

➢ We'll be resilient to criticism and less concerned about what others may or may not think about us.

➢ We won't be envious of other people or feel the need to put them down.

➢ We'll be able to let more people into our lives as they don't represent threats but potential sources of fun and learning.

➢ We'll be clear minded, less preoccupied with hurtful comparisons.

➢ We won't have the same need to prove ourselves.

➢ In short, we'll be stronger, healthier and happier.

The 'moodometer' - before and after

I've attempted to illustrate what progress will look like in the charts below. These show the stylised development of what I have called our 'moodometer', removing the effects of any seasonal factors and big one-off events. The left hand version demonstrates the current course of our psychological well-being and the right hand one how it will develop as we proceed in the direction of our Target-Selves.

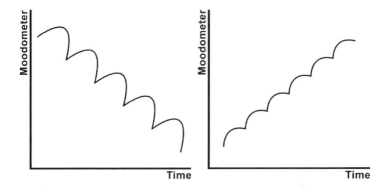

There are several observations to make. First, the lines are trending in opposite directions. This is partly designed to indicate the often self-fulfilling nature of our thoughts - by thinking that we're inferior, we'll feel inferior and by thinking we're making progress, we'll feel better and be encouraged to continue working. The improvement in the right hand chart, of course, also reflects the beneficial effects of the adjustments themselves.

In both images, the 'moodometer' is not a straight line but moves up and down. At present, we feel better about ourselves at some times than others and even when we're implementing the changes, there will be, as mentioned, setbacks along the way. We shouldn't forget that temporary ups and downs are a feature of everyday life and should be embraced as such. It would be a very dull existence without them.

Finally, the left hand 'moodometer' is more volatile than the right hand one: the extent of our ups and downs are bigger now than they will be in future. Those of us whose mood is heavily influenced by comparisons often experience a significant lift from downward comparisons and a big drop as a result of upward ones. Better comparisons coupled with a stronger sense of self-worth mean our mood swings will be less dramatic.

But what about happiness...

You may be surprised that I haven't suggested *explicitly* aiming to be 'happy' as one of our objectives. There are several reasons for this.

Happiness is a *consequence* of other things, including a better use of comparisons as I've described. Interestingly, even the head of the "Happiness Research Institute" (yes, there is such an organisation) prefers to talk about the *'happiness of pursuit'* rather than the *'pursuit of happiness'* for this reason.

Since happiness is not something we can create out of thin air, there's a danger that the more actively we search for it, the more elusive it appears to be and the unhappier we become. In some ways, it's like looking for the proverbial pot of gold at the end of the rainbow. Given that it's impossible to be permanently happy, we could consider ourselves to be failing at times when we're not happy - hardly a recipe for contentment! And, even if we try to induce happiness by bringing to mind things we believe make us happy, the danger is that we end up dwelling on the fact that we don't have them now and are no closer to getting them.

It's easy to be wrong about the causes of happiness as well. While most of us assume that we'll be happier if we have more money, for example, reality is often very different. According to the majority of research in this area, there's little or no link between money (or possessions) and happiness beyond that amount which comfortably caters for our basic requirements. How we use comparisons helps explain this phenomenon. Let's say we land a new, better paid, job. It probably won't be long before we start comparing our wage packet with colleagues who earn even more, feeling dissatisfied as a result. Additionally, the more we have of anything, including money, the less enjoyable an extra amount becomes - another £50 for Bill Gates will mean considerably less to him than it will do to somebody without a roof over their head.

If we need to think about happiness at all, it's simply (and briefly) to anticipate being *happier* as a result of the changes we're going to make.

...and self-esteem?

We would also be unwise to make 'high' self-esteem an objective in its own right. To begin with, it's not obvious what exactly is meant by high in this regard - high relative to what or whom? What we're really looking for is an internal sense of *higher* self-esteem: a recognition that we're more satisfied with our lives, more capable and have a greater respect for ourselves.

In similar fashion to happiness, we should be aware that self-esteem is a byproduct of our thought processes, often closely linked to the comparisons we make. Again, it's these thoughts that we must concentrate on adjusting if we're to experience a lasting improvement in our self-esteem.

'High' self-esteem isn't the be all and end all that some would have us believe either: it can still be associated with several negative characteristics as we discovered earlier in the chapter. Yes, higher self-esteem is necessary for a better way of living, but it's *not* sufficient to guarantee one.

In brief

At the outset of any physical journey we'll have a destination in mind and a good idea of how to get to it. The same should also be true when embarking on a mental one.

Our journey's end here is clear: stronger, healthier and happier selves. To arrive at this point we'll need to use comparisons in a very different way to now. Those that are better than us will be sources of learning and inspiration rather than triggers for envy and self-loathing. Those that are not as good as us in certain respects won't be used as vehicles to boost our ego. We'll be more empathetic instead. The comparisons we make with our past and Target-Selves will tell us how we're progressing and convince us that the journey is worth continuing.

Directly aiming to achieve happiness and high self-esteem often backfires. These should be thought of as the fruits of our endeavours rather than explicit targets that we must meet.

Chapter 6

Comparison Conditioning: The Art of Constructive Thinking

Ready to change?

It's useful to begin this chapter by reminding ourselves of what we're aiming to achieve.

1. *To be resilient to upward comparisons that will represent a genuine source of motivation and learning*

2. *To no longer rely on downward comparisons to inflate our ego*

3. *To make comparisons with our past and Target-Selves purely to monitor progress and remind ourselves of where we're heading*

So how are we going to achieve these objectives and, in so doing, move from our current-selves - the person who experiences many of the harmful thoughts and behaviours set out in chapter 4 - to the stronger, healthier and happier Target-Selves described in chapter 5? *Change* is essential.

Even if we accept that we have problems and are a long way from living the best life we can, the prospect of change can still be extremely daunting. It often feels much safer to deal with what's familiar, even though it's a long way from perfect, than cope with the unfamiliar, which *could* prove to be worse - 'better the devil you know than the devil you don't.' But perhaps the leap of faith required to make progress is not as big and scary as we might imagine.

It's important to recognise that we weren't born with the intense feelings of inferiority or superiority I described previously but have unwittingly adopted various thought patterns and associated schemas to become so. In similar fashion to the distorted image we see of ourselves when looking into a fairground mirror, our self-image and self-esteem has become warped by the faulty comparisons we have made in the past and continue to make now.

However successful we are in the changes we make, we're not suddenly going to become a different person that our friends and family won't recognise. The alterations we need to make are only those necessary to uncover a more accurate version of our true-selves: one that is not hostage to the same harmful thoughts as now. To protect ourselves, many of us have partially shut down, avoiding encounters and experiences that could enrich our lives but inevitably carry with them an element of risk to our psychological well-being. By removing the shackles imposed by our negative thoughts, we're far more likely to flourish; to realise our potential.

A CBT approach

Just as it's possible to think our way *into* problems by the way we interpret real or imaginary events, it's also perfectly possible to think our way *out* of them. To do so we need to identify our damaging thoughts, evaluate them and then reset our thinking in a more constructive direction. In so doing, we'll be able to replace our harmful thinking (and behavioural) habits with helpful ones. It's the process that lies at the heart of Cognitive Behavioural Therapy (CBT).

For those unfamiliar with CBT, the approach has several important characteristics.

> ➢ Underlying the therapy is the conviction that it's not specific events that upset us, but the meaning we attach to them that has the potential to do so. For example, when confronted by an individual who's better than us at something we have a choice - internalise the negative implications of the comparison, dismiss it as irrelevant or see it as a possible learning opportunity. The impact on our mental health will vary enormously depending on which option we take. If it's the first and we're suffering as a consequence, we can still change the effects by adjusting the meaning we originally gave to the comparison.

> ➢ There's a close *two way* relationship between our thoughts and behaviours. By thinking 'I'm really bad at small talk' (compared with everybody else), we might fidget nervously and stumble over our words when attempting to speak to others. This leads us to conclude, 'I was right. I really am terrible at this.' CBT suggests that the best chance of breaking a vicious cycle of this sort is to address both our thinking *and* our actions.

> ➢ Generally, little time is given to understanding exactly how and where our unhelpful thinking originated from. We may well have our theories but they could be wrong and, in any case, we can't reverse time to change what has already occurred. To improve our future, it's better to focus on the present - our current thought patterns and how we can modify them for the better.

> Having clear and achievable objectives, keeping them at the forefront of our minds, is crucial to remaining on track. If the ultimate goal(s) seems too far away, we need to establish more manageable, shorter-term targets as well.

> The techniques employed are sufficiently practical, understandable and transparent that we can easily implement them by ourselves to help ourselves. We should quickly gain a good enough grasp of the techniques to be able to adapt them to our specific circumstances. In effect, we become our own therapist.

CBT is widely acknowledged as a highly effective method of dealing with a range of psychological issues. I am going to use many of its principles here to tackle our comparison related problems, beginning with those associated with our upward comparisons before moving on to our downward ones.

Upward comparisons

The thought and behavioural sequence I've set out below illustrates what currently happens when we compare ourselves to others whom we deem better than us. We quickly conclude that we're inferior, telling ourselves that we're useless and feeling ashamed of our abilities. We may then behave in a submissive manner - avoiding eye contact (if it's a face-to-face interaction), agreeing with everything the other person says or just passively doing what we're told. Alternatively, we might find ourselves getting irritated, attempting to put the other individual down by picking petty holes in their arguments or appearance. In short, the upward comparison leads us to feel worse about ourselves and behave in a manner that compounds the problem.

Current Situation

I compare upwards

I believe that I'm inferior

I feel useless. I act badly

I repeat the pattern

As an example, we could compare ourselves with a colleague, concluding that we're not as popular as her. 'A lot more people know and like her than they do me. She has a huge number of friends on Facebook and gets loads of nice comments. I hardly get any. Why doesn't anybody think I'm worth knowing? There must be something wrong with me.' We're grumpy and end up arguing with our partner that evening.

While this is far from ideal, we seemingly can't stop repeating the sequence whenever we encounter the situation. Often, the process becomes so ingrained that we don't even register that we're making a comparison but simply experience the subsequent psychological pain.

To have any chance of altering this sort of destructive pattern we first need to be aware of what it is we're doing. Precisely because of the habitual nature of it, this often involves working backwards - having felt the pain we pause to think carefully about what triggered it. We could ask ourselves questions such as, 'What was going through my mind just before I began to feel this way?' or 'What images did I have when faced with the situation?' to help the process.

Once we're clearer about the triggers and sequence of events, the futility of our current thinking - the fact that all we achieve by making the upward comparisons is to feel bad about ourselves and behave poorly as a consequence - should become apparent. This represents important progress in itself.

Thereafter, our aim is *neither* to stop making upward comparisons nor to simply dismiss our negative thinking as 'wrong' but rather to rationally and calmly test the validity of our current thoughts. We'll generally find that they fail that test, prompting us to come up with more constructive alternatives.

To help guide this process, it's a good idea to write 'Thought Records'. These can take slightly different forms but I've set out the structure that I think works best below, completing it on the basis of my example.

	Thought Record - Nobody Likes Me
What was the trigger?	Seeing my colleague's Facebook page
What did I think & how did I feel?	There must be something wrong with me because she has so many more friends than I do. Nobody likes me
Is my thinking valid?	Do I have any friends? What about my family? Do they like me? Why does it matter if somebody else has more friends? Does having fewer friends mean that there's something wrong with me? Do I have qualities that people like in me?
What are some alternative, constructive thoughts?	*It's not a competition. I do have a couple of good friends* *It's the quality of friends that matters more than the quantity* *I am likeable*

Our new thoughts are shown at the bottom of the table and we need to commit them to memory so that, in future, each time we experience the hurtful thoughts we can consciously replace them with our better ones. With practise we'll be able to minimise the former by thinking the latter *ahead* of those situations that we know will prompt our hurtful comparisons.

Stage 1

I compare upwards

I believe that I'm inferior

I feel useless. I act badly...

...but I start to think my alternative, more constructive thoughts

I'm getting closer to *not* repeating the pattern

Clearly, it's not always feasible to write a Record immediately we experience a harmful thought but we should try to do so as quickly as possible. Phones with 'Notes' apps mean a pen and paper are no longer essential, while there are also specific CBT apps we can use for the purpose. As you can see from my example, there's no need to write an essay, although what we do write should be both meaningful and true to ourselves.

Progress depends critically on coming up with appropriate alternative thoughts for the situation - ones that are constructive, believable and can be supported by evidence. The new thoughts shouldn't just be positive for positive's sake but need to be realistic as well. A positive but unbelievable thought has little or no chance of helping. For instance, replacing our original thought of 'Nobody likes me' with 'I'm the most popular person in the world' is worse than worthless as we'll inevitably encounter plenty of situations that cast doubt on this.

Once we have gained an increasing awareness of our thought processes and can consider more constructive alternative thoughts, we're likely to experience something called cognitive dissonance - a state of 'psychological discomfort'. We've all had times when we hold a particular view only for it to be confounded by new information. The feeling we get then is the same as we should expect now and, although it sounds less than desirable, it represents an essential part of the improvement process. Why? Because when we hold two thoughts that are inconsistent with each other, our brain works to resolve the difference. We either reconcile the two cognitions or gradually eliminate one of them.

The good news is that by carefully evaluating our initial negative thought and (usually) finding that it lacks support we're already nudging ourselves in the direction of our alternative. Deliberately seeking and accepting evidence that supports the better thought will further improve the chances that it supersedes the poor one.

Returning to my example, let's assume that we've reached a stage when, during time spent with our 'more popular' colleague, we're sometimes convinced that nobody likes us but at other points can acknowledge our likeable qualities and the fact we have a couple of good friends. We could reconcile these conflicting thoughts by concluding 'My "friends" are just being nice because they feel sorry for me.' In this case, our original thoughts will remain with us. But by questioning these thoughts and actively recalling our constructive versions, the latter have an excellent chance of taking root and, in so doing, gradually crowding out the harmful ones.

We'll know that we've succeeded when our new thoughts become the default in relevant situations - our so-called Negative Automatic Thoughts (NATs) are supplanted by one or more Constructive Automatic Thoughts (CATs). I will say more about how we can achieve this in chapter 9.

We mustn't forget that some upward comparisons can serve a useful purpose by providing motivation and/or a method to improve. Stage 2, therefore, requires us to ask ourselves 'Can I gain anything from the comparison I'm making?' If the answer is 'Yes' then we should try to do so. For instance, 'My colleague seems to spend quite a lot of time emailing and calling her friends. It would be fun to do a bit more of that myself.' If it's a genuine 'No' then that's also fine. If, however, it's 'No, because I'm worthless' then we'll need to call upon our familiar, alternative thoughts again.

Stage 2

I compare upwards

Can I gain anything from this?

'Yes'	'No'	'No, because I'm worthless'
⬇	⬇	⬇
I learn the lessons	I move on	I think my alternative thoughts

Once we've completed this process and can deal successfully with a couple of specific situations that triggered hurtful comparisons we're likely to find that those resembling them should become much easier as well. Our aim, with practise, is to reach a position where *all* upward comparisons can only have two possible outcomes - we either gain something helpful from them or we move on because there's nothing that *can* be gained. Crucially, our hurtful, inferior thoughts are no longer triggered by such comparisons: we don't feel a sense of threat when using them in *any* circumstances. In time we may even learn to stop making upward comparisons where we're unlikely to receive any benefit from them, reserving them for more promising situations. This is the third and final Stage and, once there, we'll have met the first of our key objectives.

Stage 3

I compare upwards...

...to learn and feel motivated by it

Looking at Stage 3 you may be wondering why we carefully chose and practised alternative thoughts when we don't end up using them here. Why not miss out this step? The answer is that they're an essential part of eliminating our entrenched negative thoughts. If we don't work hard to replace them, we'll risk a relapse whenever we compare upwards.

Downward comparisons

If we're frequently comparing downwards to make ourselves feel superior to others then we also have a problem, particularly if our resulting thoughts spill over into arrogant actions.

To some, it may not seem like much of an issue but I would beg to differ. As I pointed out earlier, repeatedly trying to pump ourselves up at the expense of others likens us to bullies. It may boost our ego, but it can have detrimental effects on the psychological well-being of others, irrespective of whether that's our intention. It can make us lazy and careless as well, failing to anticipate or prepare properly for situations. Although it's perfectly possible to gain admirers by behaving in a superior manner I suggest that these are not the sort of friends that stick around. Their loyalty is likely to be found wanting when it becomes apparent that we're not quite as brilliant as we would have them believe.

We should also understand that the effect of downward comparisons of this sort can be addictive. In similar fashion to a nicotine rush, while they may temporarily improve our mood the impact will become shorter and shorter each time. If we're not careful we'll find ourselves needing to make increasing numbers of these comparisons to receive the same psychological boost.

My conclusion? We must kick the habit. Of course, acknowledging that we have a downward comparison problem is not necessarily going to be straightforward. But for the sake of healthy relationships as well as our psychological well-being it's crucial to be honest with ourselves. We also need to listen to what others, whom we respect, are telling us about our behaviour.

Current Situation

I compare downwards

I believe that I'm superior

I briefly feel good about myself...

...sometimes behaving arrogantly as a result

I repeat the pattern

Once we've decided to act, our first step, as before, is to evaluate our superior thinking and come up with more appropriate thoughts, preferably through the use of a Thought Record. Let's assume that our most frequent superior thought is 'I'm one of the best historians in the country.' In this case, our Record might look something like this.

	Thought Record - The Best Historian
What was the trigger?	Reading another historian's work
What did I think & how did I feel?	I'm one of the best historians in the country. I felt superior to the author
Is my thinking valid?	How would I measure that? Do I know every historian in the country? Do I know everything there is to know about history? Where does that thought get me? What would other historians think if they knew this? Am I just doing this to feel better about myself, and, if so, why?
What are some alternative, constructive thoughts?	*It's important to keep improving* *I can do better work in the future* *It's a huge subject. I can learn a lot from fellow historians*

Assuming our alternative thoughts are both credible and constructive then, with plenty of repetition, they will initially temper and eventually dominate our original thought in the same manner that I described previously. I have shown what Stage 1 looks like overleaf.

Stage 1

I compare downwards

I believe that I'm superior

I briefly feel good about myself...

...but I start to think my alternative, more constructive thoughts

I'm getting closer to *not* repeating the pattern

Again, this is not to suggest that we give up making downward comparisons altogether. Rather, as with upward comparisons, we should be very clear about their proper purpose and hence their appropriate use. I noted earlier that downward comparisons can help create empathy as well as providing a handy means of checking our progress. By providing a way to evaluate ourselves relative to others, they can also be useful when we need to assign responsibilities when tackling a joint task. For example, if two historians are tasked with writing a book, one may say, 'I know more about this period than you,' while the second suggests 'I've done more in-depth research in the other area.' As a result, they are now better placed to split the work.

With this in mind and having improved our thinking for a couple of particular situations, Stage 2 involves posing a question when we find ourselves making downward comparisons - 'Why am I doing this?' If it's designed to assert superiority we should resort to appropriate alternative thoughts, while if it's for a more constructive reason then there's no need to do so.

Stage 2

I compare downwards

Why am I doing this?

Constructive   **Destructive**

↓   ↓

I feel empathy, monitor my progress or allocate tasks   **I think my alternative thoughts**

Once we've beaten our desire to make downward comparisons for destructive reasons, we'll find ourselves in Stage 3 - only making them for the three purposes I have described. In so doing, we'll have achieved our second objective.

Stage 3

I compare downwards...

...to feel empathy, monitor my progress or allocate tasks

There *is* an alternative

The precise situations in which our (upward and downward) comparisons lead us to feel worse about ourselves or superior to others will vary enormously from person to person. Nevertheless, I have come up with some generic, constructive thoughts in the next few pages that hopefully you'll be able to adapt to your specific circumstances. My focus here is dealing with the harmful thoughts, beliefs and assumptions I listed at the beginning of chapter 4. For each 'Case' I have included questions designed to challenge the validity of our current thinking and elicit new thoughts. Many of the questions and alternative thoughts are relevant to more than one of the Cases.

Case 1

Thought/Belief/Assumption/Schema Triggered by Comparison

I'm useless

Questions to Help Evaluation

o   Am I making a fair comparison?
o   What makes me think that?
o   What's the evidence for and against?
o   Have I had other experiences that suggest this is untrue?
o   Could I look at this in another, more constructive, way?
o   Am I jumping to conclusions not supported by the facts?
o   What would I say to a good friend thinking this?
o   What would a good friend say to me?
o   Am I helping myself or making things worse by thinking like this?

Possible Alternative Thoughts

o   This is just a thought, it's not reality.
o   The comparison is unfair and there's no point making it.
o   I've achieved many positive things in my life.
o   I have strengths and good points.
o   Several people like me.
o   I can and do help others.
o   I'm better than I used to be and will continue to improve.
o   I remember situations when I didn't feel like this. I can do that again.

Case 2

Thought/Belief/Assumption/Schema Triggered by Comparison

I have to be the best at everything I do

Questions to Help Evaluation

- Is it realistic to be the best at everything?
- What would happen if I wasn't the best?
- What's the worst that will happen if I'm not the best?
- Will I remember whether I won or lost in a couple of months?
- Why does being the best matter so much to me? Is it for my benefit or somebody else's?
- Will the people who matter really think worse of me if I'm not the best at everything?
- What do other people think of me behaving the way I am?
- What would I think of somebody determined to win even the most minor of contests?

Possible Alternative Thoughts

- Everybody has strengths and weaknesses.
- Being bad at something doesn't define me as a person.
- I can only be the best I can be.
- I'm not the best, but that's okay.
- I don't need to prove myself.
- It's impossible to be the best at everything. Nobody has been, is or ever will be.
- In most situations, it doesn't matter if I'm the best or not.
- I'm missing out on experiences by avoiding those where I won't be the best.
- I'm going to be less serious and laugh at my mistakes.
- I'll be more likeable if I'm not always set on being the best.

Case 3

Thought/Belief/Assumption/Schema Triggered by Comparison

I'm so envious of other people's looks and abilities. I wish I could be them

Questions to Help Evaluation

○ Is the person I'm comparing myself with really that perfect?
○ Am I seeing the whole picture or just a partial, biased impression?
○ Could I make more of an effort to improve my appearance and feel better about myself?
○ What would friends say to me if I told them I was envious of them or somebody else?
○ What would I say to a friend who said they were envious of me?
○ Would my friends and family want me to be somebody completely different?
○ Can I learn from other people who have dealt with the same thoughts & feelings?

Possible Alternative Thoughts

○ Everybody has weaknesses and worries.
○ I have my own unique set of qualities and plenty of people like me for those.
○ There's a few easy things I can do that will make me look better and feel more satisfied.
○ There are far more important things in life than looking attractive.
○ I am who I am and that's fine by me.

Case 4

Thought/Belief/Assumption/Schema Triggered by Comparison

Others are making hurtful comparisons about me

Questions to Help Evaluation

- What's the evidence that the other person is making a harmful comparison?
- Is my interpretation of the other person's reaction correct?
- Are there other possible interpretations of the situation?
- Are their possible thoughts, beliefs or assumptions about me correct?
- Are their expectations of me too high?
- Does it matter what they think?

Possible Alternative Thoughts

- It's a waste of my time to worry about what others may or may not be thinking.
- If they're thinking like that about me then they are wrong to do so.
- If they don't think much of me, then that's their problem not mine.
- If they feel better about themselves having made the comparison then that's okay.
- It's up to me whether I'm hurt by the comparison or not. I don't have to be.
- I'm not the first person to fail or make a mistake. I can apologise (if appropriate), learn and move on.

Case 5

Thought/Belief/Assumption/Schema Triggered by Comparison

I may have won but I'm not a success

Questions to Help Evaluation

- ○ Did I have to work hard to win?
- ○ Did the other person/team want to win?
- ○ Would other people want to have achieved what I've achieved?
- ○ Would they classify me as a 'success'?
- ○ What is my goal and am I getting closer to achieving it?
- ○ How am I defining success? Am I being realistic?
- ○ What's wrong with enjoying my win/success?

Possible Alternative Thoughts

- ○ I would have felt badly about myself if I had lost, so I'll enjoy my win.
- ○ I know I have a long way to go to reach my goals but I'm moving in the right direction.
- ○ There are plenty of ups and downs in life. I'm going to enjoy the ups and learn from the downs.
- ○ I'm lucky to have people who want me to succeed. My joy is a way of giving back and a good chance to thank them for their support.

Case 6

Thought/Belief/Assumption/Schema Triggered by Comparison

Other people's successes are my failures. I can't enjoy them

Questions to Help Evaluation

- What is it that makes me feel badly about myself if somebody else succeeds?
- What do I gain by thinking this way?
- Wouldn't it be better to enjoy the successes of the people I care for?
- What do other people think of me if I look miserable when they succeed?

Possible Alternative Thoughts

- Others' successes don't take anything away from me.
- I've had my successes and will have more in the future. It's their turn now.
- This is not about me, it's about them.
- There's enough doom and gloom in the world. Let's take every chance to celebrate.
- They worked hard to achieve what they have. It's right to be pleased for them. They deserve it.

Case 7

Thought/Belief/Assumption/Schema Triggered by Comparison

I'm so much better than everybody else

Questions to Help Evaluation

- o   Is this factually correct?
- o   What would those people I'm comparing myself with think about me if they knew?
- o   What do I think of people behaving arrogantly?
- o   This helps me feel better about myself but how long does the feeling last?
- o   Am I helping or hurting others by thinking and behaving in a superior way?

- o   Possible Alternative Thoughts

- o   There's always room for improvement.
- o   There are people better than me and I can learn from them.
- o   Modesty is a positive trait that I like in others and others will like in me.
- o   The only person I should try to be better than is the person I was yesterday.
- o   The people who care for me know my strengths (and weaknesses). I don't need to keep telling them.

Comparisons with our past and Target-Selves

The third and final objective - 'To make comparisons with our past and Target-Selves purely to monitor progress and remind ourselves of where we're heading' - is the most straightforward of the three to meet.

The key is to remember to do it, particularly when doubts about the process surface. Also, the downward comparisons we make with our past-selves mustn't trigger complacency but confidence, while the upward comparisons with our Target-Selves are designed to motivate rather than intimidate.

In brief

Achieving our comparison related ambitions will require plenty of dedication and hard work. Partly through the use of Thought Records, we need to crystallise our unhelpful thoughts, invalidate them where possible, come up with constructive alternatives and then actively practise thinking these new thoughts.

In this way we'll be well placed to make upward and downward comparisons only when they help ourselves or others. Comparisons that were once destructive will become constructive, freeing us from many previous constraints and easing our psychological pain. We'll be able to live a richer, more enjoyable life as a consequence.

Chapter 7

Acceptance, Action Plans & Dealing with Failure

What if our hurtful thinking is right?

So far I have looked at how we can adjust our thinking in response to upward and downward comparisons that trigger *invalid* beliefs about ourselves and harm our mental well-being in the process.

While this method will resolve most situations, there are occasions when it won't work. In challenging our current thinking it's possible that we conclude - *with complete justification* - that we're very bad at something or worse than others in some way. We might determine, for example, 'It isn't a problem of my perception but a stone-cold fact that I'm overweight. After all, I'm 50% heavier than the UK average for people of my gender and height.' In these circumstances, are our harmful thoughts and behaviours correct and therefore unavoidable? In short, no.

<u>Current Situation</u>

I compare upwards

I believe that I'm inferior

I test my belief and find it's correct

I feel worse. I act badly

I repeat the pattern

Earlier, I argued that there's no point thinking alternative thoughts that are evidently wrong. Hence, in the circumstances I've just described, trying to convince ourselves that, 'I'm actually quite thin' won't achieve anything. Even saying to ourselves 'I'm still lighter than some people' is unlikely to be particularly helpful. The more appropriate response will vary depending on whether we want to change and can do so.

Assuming that we're not content with our current situation and are able to do something about it, we'll need to come up with an *Action Plan*. 'I know I'm overweight now but I am going to work hard to lose some kgs. Rather than exercise once a week for half an hour, I'll go to the gym three times and try to extend each workout to 40 minutes. I'm also going to cut out ice cream for a month and see what difference that makes.' Our plans need to be dynamic, adapting to the progress we are (or are not) making.

If, having completed our Action Plan and successfully met our objectives, we still believe that we have a problem then we'll need to implement the strategies detailed in the previous chapter.

There may also be situations where we decide, for whatever reason, that we would rather remain as we are. Here, *Constructive Acceptance* is vital. This involves acknowledging our current circumstances, while generating and thinking valid, positive thoughts that will help overcome the psychological hurt associated with our comparisons. For my example, this could be 'Yes, I am overweight, but that doesn't define me as a person' or 'So what if I'm heavier than most. Who cares?' We'll know that we're making progress when the frequency of our comparisons decline and they don't generate the pain they used to.

Finally, what if we would like to change our circumstances but can't? 'I'm stupid! My IQ is lower than my peers and the national average and there's nothing I can do to alter that.' In these circumstances we must again *Constructively Accept* the situation, thinking ourselves into a better place. 'Okay, I have a relatively low IQ but that doesn't mean I'm stupid. There are all sorts of different types of intelligence - emotional, sporting, driving, gardening etc. I'm good at one or two of these.' Another thought could be 'Those with the highest IQ aren't always the most popular or financially successful people. I'm still perfectly capable of doing well in life.'

Stage 1

I compare upwards

I believe that I'm inferior

I test my belief and find it's correct

I practise Constructive Acceptance or I adopt an Action Plan

I'm getting closer to *not* repeating the pattern

In time, we won't compare upwards in the same way as before as we'll either have achieved what we want to achieve through our Action Plan or have come to terms psychologically with our situation.

Dealing with mistakes, losses and failures

We need to consider the fall-out from one final set of circumstances involving comparisons. When we lose, make a mistake or fail at something we often make hurtful comparisons - relating our current situation to the success of others or what might have been if we hadn't flunked it.

Somebody may say to us, for example, 'You were wrong to write that email. If you had only listened to me you wouldn't be in the trouble you are now.' Alternatively we could think, 'If I had just read the questions properly I would have passed the exam and been able to go to a better college' or 'By practising harder, I wouldn't have lost that game.' Our thoughts and actions are ones of regret, frustration or anger, usually involving the words 'if only', either explicitly or implicitly.

<u>**Current Situation**</u>

I've made a mistake or failed

I make a hurtful comparison

I feel worse

I avoid the situation or repeat the pattern

Even though blunders are a frequent and unavoidable part of everyday life we're typically very bad at dealing with them, generally responding in one or more of the following ways...

➢ We keep reminding ourselves of our mistakes, triggering hurtful thoughts and feelings.

➤ We avoid situations that replicate or resemble those we've failed at.

➤ We blame some external factor, such as bad luck, for our failure.

None of these actions, barring successful avoidance, will help prevent us from repeating the error in the future.

So what's the alternative? Our constructive thinking approach suggests that we should neither ignore nor dwell on our failings but establish a better routine - one which removes the negative thoughts and emotion from the situation and allows us to learn from the experience *if* that's appropriate. The method, closely linked to several of the techniques I have already described, is set out below.

Stage 1

I've made a mistake or failed

Can I learn from this?

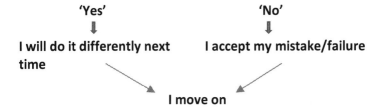

Having made a mistake, lost or failed we need to ask ourselves whether there is anything we can take from the experience. If there is, then we should mentally store what we have learnt, retrieving it when next faced with the same or similar situation. That way we'll reduce the chance of making it again. If there isn't then we should accept what's happened and dismiss the memory. (Whatever our conclusion, we may also want to apologise to anybody who has been adversely affected by our mistake or failure!)

This is easier to write than to do and unfortunately there's no shortcut to repeating the sequence until it becomes ingrained. Whenever our mind wanders back to the mistake we'll need return to the beginning of the process.

Let's assume that we've failed an interview for a new job, leading us to think badly about ourselves - 'If only my answers had been better than those of the other candidates I would have landed that position and achieved a big pay rise.' Rather than let this thought linger, convincing ourselves that we're a failure and will never get another job, we ask ourselves 'What could I do differently at my next interview?' Our conclusion may be 'I should learn more about the company and work on calming my nerves.' With these thoughts now tucked away we get on with the rest of our day.

It's essential to be honest with ourselves here. It's no good blaming bad luck, for example, if this is not the real reason for our failure, while avoidance is unlikely to be the answer either.

At the same time, we shouldn't spend hours analysing the minutia of our mistakes. Quickly learn the lesson(s) and move on. Try and let go of all the hurtful thoughts and memories. Talking on "Mind Games" (a Sky Sports documentary) ex England cricketer Darren Gough described how he deals with a bad day as follows - *'Write it, read it, rip it. Pint of Tetley's love. Done.'* It's not a bad mantra, assuming you enjoy the occasional beer!

Equipped now with a far better way of dealing with failure, our *fear* of failing will diminish. And this, in turn, will improve our chances of success. After all, thinking about failing ties up valuable mental resources that are far better deployed working out how to succeed. We wouldn't choose to hop on one leg as an able-bodied person competing in a running race so why disadvantage ourselves mentally when faced with a challenge?

If our perception is that we're 'failing' *most* of the time we should check that we're not making inappropriate comparisons and setting our expectations too high as a result. This can happen for the reasons I discussed at the beginning of the book but is also common when our circumstances change. Take somebody who is a high-achieving student at school, used to scooping all the plaudits and prizes on offer. If that individual then attends a good university she might discover that she's no longer the best, testing a core belief she holds about herself. As we've learnt, these more fundamental problems are best resolved by changing the nature of the comparisons we make with others.

In brief

There are instances when it's impossible to invalidate our comparison related, hurtful thoughts because, well, they're true. But this doesn't mean that we need remain trapped in an endless cycle of comparisons and psychological pain. Plenty of escape routes exist.

If we're willing and able to improve our situation we should commit to a carefully considered, achievable Action Plan, checking our progress along the way. If instead, we're prepared to live with the particular issue, at least for the time being, or are simply unable to fix it, we should practise Constructive Accceptance. This involves generating constructive thoughts and making a habit of thinking them.

Mistakes and failures, meanwhile, are an unavoidable and important part of life. Rather than dwell on them we need to quickly learn the lessons, if any, and move on. Once we know how to deal effectively with failure, situations we previously avoided will seem far less threatening.

Chapter 8

Constructive Behaviours

In the last two chapters I concentrated on the importance of changing our *thought* patterns to benefit our psychological well-being as well as improve our behavioural responses to situations. There has been extensive research demonstrating that it also works the other way round: by altering our behaviour we can improve our thinking and mood.

There are many tried and tested behavioural techniques that can support our cognitive efforts and I shall describe several of them in what follows. No doubt some will prove more useful than others but I suggest all of them are worth trying.

Don't dwell, do

It's very easy to sit back and dwell on everything bad in our lives, how unfortunate we are or what's gone wrong, letting those thoughts drag our mood lower as well as reinforcing our negative schemas. If initially we can't think of anything more constructive to counterbalance such thoughts then the starting point is to *do* something, virtually anything, as long as it's not destructive.

When we need to write something and struggle to know how to begin, a good piece of advice is to scribble down the first thing of relevance that comes to mind as though we were saying it out loud. It doesn't matter if it's not very good because it can be improved at a later stage. The important thing is that we've made a start. Something similar applies when our negativity begins to overwhelm us - get up and get doing. What exactly it is, is far less important than to *stop* thinking our hurtful thoughts. It only represents a short-term fix but it's a helpful one when we're feeling trapped by our thoughts.

Exposure

CBT advocates 'Behavioural Experiments', otherwise known as 'Exposure Therapy', to help overcome a range of issues. Rather than avoid challenging situations, the idea is to actively expose ourselves to them in a controlled fashion to test our negative beliefs. If, as is likely, we find the beliefs to be inaccurate, the 'dangers' we associate with such situations may subside until, eventually, we're able to handle them perfectly well. The procedure is particularly effective in overcoming phobias, such as fears of confined spaces, spiders or heights, but can also be useful in other circumstances.

Let's say we have an intense fear of large social gatherings because of the harmful comparisons they trigger, and want to improve how we feel in such situations. Our Exposure Therapy might initially involve meeting up with one or two people we know well and are comfortable with at a local coffee house for a quick drink. Once we feel at ease doing this, we invite them to our house for a snack, perhaps with a couple of additional friends. Subsequently, we accept some return invitations and start engaging with a few people we're less familiar with, keeping calm in the process (see below). When ready, we organise a bigger party at our own house. If we can achieve all this without major issues, our thoughts will improve and we should ultimately be able to attend large get-togethers without coming away feeling miserable about ourselves.

How about if we're excessively competitive, feeling the need to put people down in conversation? We might begin by simply observing what others do in these situations - 'Are they attempting to score points and, if so, how does that make me feel about them?' Later, when involved in conversations and finding that we're up to our old tricks we ask ourselves 'What do I achieve by doing this? How is my "target" likely to feel and will other people be impressed by my actions?' We consciously adopt a friendlier, more collaborative approach, while noting how we feel in the process. As always, actively practising our new method until it becomes second nature is crucial.

Composure

There are big advantages to be had in achieving poise during challenging situations, be they face-to-face or larger-scale interactions, communicating electronically with others or even when we're alone with our hurtful thoughts and want to come up with better ones. By thinking calmly under pressure, we're far more likely to successfully manage the issue(s) at hand. This doesn't mean that we'll always resolve them to our and everybody else's satisfaction but we will at least give ourselves the best chance of doing so. To achieve this we must learn to quieten the anxiety that so frequently accompanies these situations.

For evolutionary reasons, our brains are hypersensitive to danger and it's largely for this reason that we experience anxiety. But while being alert to potential jeopardy was extremely useful to our distant ancestors who faced frequent life-threatening situations it's less helpful now. In the vast majority of circumstances, we don't require the natural physiological and cognitive reactions that see our heart rates rise, muscles tighten, breathing quicken and minds 'contract'. The classic 'fight or flight response' is generally inappropriate these days and we need ways to counter it, either by reframing threats or improving our ability to cope with their effects.

Two types of anxiety exist - State and Trait. The former is what we experience when faced with a specific threat (be it real or perceived) and the latter a more generalised, enduring sense of unease. Here, I'm primarily interested in how to deal with State anxiety as many of the techniques I detailed in the last two chapters, as well as those I will explore in the next one, should help us overcome Trait related worries.

There are many ways to calm our body and mind and we'll need to experiment to discover which ones work best for us. Below, I have focused on those that are quick, simple and subtle, bearing in mind that we may require their use when in public. They represent a mixture of physical and cognitive suggestions.

➢ *Diaphragmatic breathing* is probably the most effective physical technique that suits the conditions I have set. It simply involves breathing slowly and deeply by contracting the diaphragm: inhaling through the nose and exhaling through the mouth. We can test whether we're doing it correctly by placing one had on our stomach and the other on our chest: the former should rise and fall as we breath in and out while the latter shouldn't move. Such breathing slows our heart rate, lowers our blood pressure and allows us to get more oxygen to the brain. Some suggest that it also reduces levels of the stress hormone cortisol. We can combine this approach with many of those that follow.

➢ *Muscle relaxation* is another popular method. Ideally, it involves lying down in a quiet, comfortable, dark location, before tightening each muscle individually for about 10 seconds and then relaxing for 20 seconds. As we slowly relax the muscle, we 'see' the tension leaving our body to be replaced with a sense of warmth, security and calm. The more convenient version is to progressively tighten our whole body, starting with our toes and moving up to our head, before letting all the tension go at once. It can be completed in a matter of seconds.

➢ By imagining ourselves in a place where we feel relaxed and confident, filling in the picture with as much detail as possible, we can coax our mind and body into believing that we're there. The more convincing our *visualisation* the calmer we'll feel. Just as sportspeople visualise themselves performing to the best of their abilities and winning, positive mental imagery can provide powerful support in our quest for improvement.

➢ *Setting appropriate expectations* is important. By seeking perfection we're likely to try too hard and be excessively critical on ourselves when making any sort of mistake - hardly a recipe for calmness and success. Better thoughts are 'I can only be as good as I can be,' 'I'm going to give this my best shot and see where that gets me' or 'I want to come out of this with no regrets.' As the saying goes, 'refuse to let the perfect be the enemy of the good.'

➢ Sports psychologists emphasise the importance of *controlling the controllables* as opposed to concerning ourselves with things that we can't influence. A striker in football should concentrate on getting into the best position to score a goal instead of fretting about the crowd, for example. We can easily extend this technique to a variety of non-sporting situations. During an interview, for instance, our focus should be on answering the questions to the best of our ability, not worrying about what the person sitting opposite is thinking about us or how we will rank relative to the other candidates.

➤ *Focusing on the process not the outcome* represents similar advice, again most commonly used in a sporting context but with wider benefits. The idea here is that we shouldn't cast our mind forward to what may or may not happen as a result of our actions but concentrate on the actions themselves. Let's say we're facing a tight deadline to write a report for our boss and find ourselves worrying about his reaction to it - 'He's going to hate this and think badly about me as a result.' Rather than occupying our minds with thoughts that make this negative outcome more probable, we should get deeply involved in the report itself - 'How I can improve this to give it more meaning? Are there any examples I can use to strengthen the argument? Is there a chart I could draw that would make things clearer?'

➤ Silently repeating a calming or encouraging *mantra*, preferably in a meditative way, helps many. Examples include 'I can because I think I can,' 'I believe in myself,' 'I am powerful and capable' and 'Everything I need is within me.' This has similarities to the constructive thinking approach of the last chapter and indeed our mantra could be the thought we have come up with. A good mantra should be short, personally meaningful and provide an instant positive message.

➤ *Distraction* is a useful way to stop thinking our anxious thoughts. Instead of worrying about what could go wrong in a particular situation, we focus our attention on what we can gain from it, how we can enjoy ourselves or whether there's anything we can do to help others. In conversation, we should concentrate on what the other person is saying and doing, not what we're thinking about ourselves or what they may be thinking about us. Even briefly switching our attention to the sights and sounds that surround us can be helpful.

➢ A *sense of perspective* is helpful in angst-ridden situations, serving to take pressure off our shoulders. For the reasons I explained earlier, we often overreact to perceived threats, implying that it's often useful to re-evaluate the actual degree of 'danger' involved. We could ask ourselves questions such as 'Realistically, what's the worst that could happen here?', 'Does this really matter in the grand scheme of things?' or 'Is anybody going to remember this in a week or two?'

➢ In similar vein to the last point, *cognitive distancing* involves seeing our worries as guesses not cast iron facts - they are the consequences of our mind anticipating dangers that almost certainly won't materialise. Winston Churchill put it as follows, *'When I look back on all these worries, I remember the story of the old man who said on his deathbed that he had had a lot of trouble in his life, most of which had never happened.'*

Act confident, feel confident

There are many forms of body language that we can use to convince ourselves (and others) that we feel comfortable and confident in any situation.

When experiencing feelings of inferiority it's helpful to consciously keep our heads up. Rather than hunching our shoulders and looking down, we look up, take in as much of our surroundings as possible and meet other people's eyes with all the confidence we can muster. As Helen Keller, American author and political activist, said, *'Never bend your head. Always hold it high. Look the world straight in the eye.'* In priming our senses and feeling stronger within ourselves we'll improve the likelihood of making a success of the situation.

Other classic examples of positive body language include a firm handshake, smiling when appropriate, keeping an open posture and taking up space by standing or sitting with our legs slightly apart. At the same time, we should avoid negative body language. This includes repeatedly touching our face, picking at something, tapping our hands or feet, invading other people's space, sitting on the edge of our seat or blinking frequently. Such actions are distracting and will reinforce the sense that we're ill at ease.

Slow down

There are often psychological (and practical) benefits to be had from walking and talking more slowly than we usually do in stressful circumstances. Not only will we be able to complete certain tasks more effectively than previously but, as strange as it sounds, more quickly as well sometimes.

When walking to a meeting at a client's office once, a colleague told me to 'Stop rushing!' I didn't even realise that I was, presumably because it had become the norm for me. Having slowed down, I was amazed by the effects - I felt calmer, in greater control and far more aware of everything around me. I would strongly encourage you to try it!

On another occasion, I was speaking at a conference where, after every sentence, I had to wait for my words to be translated into Japanese (which sounds very grand but wasn't). I knew this was going to happen before starting the talk and was convinced that I wouldn't be able to finish in time. After all, I had given the same presentation in English on many previous occasions and frequently overrun. I was wrong, concluding with a few minutes to spare.

I realised subsequently that by simplifying my English and having more time to contemplate what I was going to say, I must have cut out a huge number of extraneous words. I'm not suggesting that we pause for protracted periods during normal conversation, but talking a little more slowly brings a calmness to proceedings, helping us think and speak more adeptly. Earlier, I wrote about social situations where, by worrying about the impression we're making, we ensure that we don't make a particularly good one, thereby convincing ourselves that we were right to be concerned. This technique can play a part in breaking that vicious cycle.

A problem shared...

It can be advantageous to open up to those that we're close to (as well as professionals) about our problems. Apart from anything else, verbalising our difficulties often gives us a better understanding of them as well as a chance of receiving helpful advice, particularly from those who have experienced similar issues. It may have other effects as well.

A 2014 research paper investigated the impact of sharing a problem on *stress levels*.[1] 52 undergraduates at a US university were paired at random and asked to deliver a speech that would be video-recorded. The participants were encouraged to discuss how they felt about the task with their partner - their level of cortisol being measured before, during and after the talk.

The researchers found that a person fearful or public speaking could lower their stress response by speaking to somebody who was emotionally similar to them. In contrast, interacting with somebody who was emotionally different generally served to raise their stress levels. Other research has found that emotionally similar people have greater empathy for one another, experience less conflict and cooperate better, potentially explaining the results. Knowing that we're not alone in feeling the way we're feeling no doubt provides reassurance as well.

Triggering endorphins

Endorphins are a hormone produced naturally in the brain that serve to reduce our perception of pain and lift our mood, making us feel more positive and energised. There are several things we can do to stimulate their release.

- Exercise

Exercise is perhaps the most well-known trigger, although there are some subtleties, relating to the amount and intensity of activity undertaken, to keep in mind.

A 2017 Finnish study[2] found that while an hour of 'high intensity interval training' led to a significant increase in the release of endorphins, *'this appeared to be linked to increased negative feelings and pain.'* In contrast, participants in the experiment reported feelings of *'euphoria and pleasure'* following an hour of 'moderately intensive aerobic activity' that generated a smaller increase in endorphins.

The secret, therefore, seems to be to find a happy medium - neither doing so much exercise that we're utterly exhausted by it nor so little that additional endorphins (and other chemicals, including serotonin) fail to be produced.

Many studies have stressed the importance of *regular* exercise for our mental health. By increasing serotonin levels in the brain, in similar fashion to the operation of most antidepressants, it provides a long-lasting boost to our mood and general sense of well-being. Habitual exercise can also reduce stress by helping balance our body's level of adrenaline and similar hormones. According to Dr. Kip Matthews, a leading Sport and Performance Psychologist, *'By exercising frequently for a longer duration, the body becomes a lot more efficient at handling other types of stress that are put on the body.'*

There are indirect advantages to be had from frequent aerobic exercise as well. We're likely to feel more confident about our appearance, strength and resilience; it can provide a useful distraction from our harmful thoughts; and, if we choose to exercise with others, we may enjoy social benefits. If it's possible to do so, exercising shortly before an event we're worried about can be particularly beneficial. By allowing us to combine some of these indirect effects with the endorphin rush we'll be able to manage the situation better.

- Laughter

Laughter is generally accepted to have similar endorphin-inducing effects as exercise, perhaps partly because it's a form of physical activity itself. Of course, a brief laugh now and again is not going to have much effect, but if we can make it a regular feature of our day to day lives then mental (and physical) benefits should flow. I will discuss how we might do this in the next chapter.

Apart from lifting our mood and reducing our stress by creating an endorphin rush, shared laughter will serve to strengthen existing relationships and help create new ones. If used appropriately, good humour can also assist us in dealing effectively with conflict and tension. It's more difficult to be annoyed with somebody who greets people with a genuine, friendly smile, for example.

- Foods & meditation

Consumption of dark chocolate and hot chillies, even in small quantities, has been found to boost endorphin levels - the 'active' ingredients within these foods being cocoa and capsicum respectively. The mood-enhancing effects of eating these items will only be temporary, however, and while we could partake of them more regularly, the danger is that problems for our *physical* health could follow!

Meditation may also have endorphin enhancing properties and I note that it's possible to enrol for classes specifically designed to stimulate the hormone. Instead of trying to empty our mind, the idea here is that we should fill it with pleasurable thoughts. Irrespective of whether it works in the way suggested, many people find that this and other forms of meditation provide relaxation and a general sense of improved psychological well-being.

In brief

Thoughts and behaviours are mutually reinforcing, meaning that there are big advantages to be had in backing up our cognitive efforts with constructive actions. As I've described here, the latter take many different forms, from deliberately putting ourselves in tricky situations to sharing problems. Learning to cope better with our anxiety is particularly important.

Some of the techniques will be more useful than others, partly depending on the situation we find ourselves in. The secret is to work out which work best as we go about our everyday lives. Having done so, their regular use will provide a further means of progressing towards our Target-Selves.

Chapter 9

Staying the Course: Creating Habits & Building Self-Worth

Doubling down

By combining our constructive thinking approach with the behavioural techniques I outlined in the last chapter we'll make significant strides towards our objectives. Inevitably, however, there will be setbacks and doubts along the way that we must overcome to succeed. In this chapter I look at two powerful methods that can improve our chances of staying the course.

1. **Turn our new thoughts into new habits.** I've argued that if we're going to improve we must learn to replace our damaging thoughts and behaviours with constructive alternatives. The trouble is old habits die hard: it's very easy to slip back into our past, hurtful ways of thinking, particularly when presented with those situations that triggered them. We may then convince ourselves that we're failing - that our new thoughts will never supersede our hurtful ones - and give up. Unfortunately, the nature of our inferiority problems means that we're particularly vulnerable to this. We'll be much better placed, therefore, if we can convert our constructive thoughts into habits as quickly as possible.

2. **Strengthen our underlying sense of self-worth.** Given that our self-worth has been squashed by years, if not decades, of harmful upward comparisons we'll need to rebuild it, ensuring that it can withstand knocks and shocks. Ego-boosting downward comparisons shouldn't be used to achieve this for the reasons described earlier.

Creating habits - out with the old, in with the new

Most of the habits we've developed over time are incredibly useful, allowing us to function effectively as human beings. Without them, our brains would be swamped by the minutiae of everyday life as we have to think our way through how to get dressed, tie our shoelaces, clean our teeth, drive the car etc. Once the necessary processes are learnt, they occur automatically when triggered, saving us time and allowing us to focus on other things. The trouble is, as we go through life we don't just pick up good habits but bad ones as well.

Habits normally take the following form:

Trigger - Routine - Reward

If we're a nail-biter, for example, the *trigger* may be boredom, leading our brains to search automatically for the appropriate *routine* - biting our finger nails in this case - which in turn provides a *reward* - relief from the boredom and perhaps a pleasurable sensation. The reward encourages us to repeat the experience when the same situation arises and so the 'habit loop' continues. In many instances, we'll begin to anticipate and crave the reward, strengthening the habit further.

For most of our harmful thinking habits, while the trigger and routine is usually clear, the reward is not (the exception being downward comparisons that generate a sense of superiority). But if there's nothing to be gained from those upward comparisons that create feelings of inferiority, why have they seemingly become habitual? The reason is that making such comparisons and reacting to them badly was the *only* way we knew how to respond in certain situations. Having established our constructive thoughts and behaviours we now have an alternative.

Experts argue that the best method of replacing a bad habit with a good one is to leave the trigger and reward the same but change the routine.[1] As I've made clear, our position is slightly different: when making upward comparisons there was no reward to begin with, only hurt, while we no longer want the same reward (feelings of superiority) when making downward comparisons.

The good news is that our new routine - thinking our constructive thoughts in potentially troublesome situations – will start to bring rewards along the lines described in chapter 5. And these in turn will inspire us to continue. Meanwhile, our revised reaction to downward comparisons will still yield benefits, albeit very different ones to before. Instead of feeling superior we'll experience greater empathy. As such, we should now have the necessary ingredients to form better, healthier habits.

Nevertheless, there's still a lot more we can do to reinforce the process.

➢ *Memorise our constructive thoughts.* If this is proving problematic, we could jot them down on 'stickies', which we place in obvious positions such as the bathroom mirror or the inside of the door we leave the house by to remind us of what they are.

➢ *Set aside some time every day to rehearse our new thoughts*, mentally putting ourselves in challenging situations and thinking our way out of them. This need only be for five minutes while we're in the shower, getting dressed or, best of all, just before we go to sleep. Ideally, we should practise in the same place at roughly the same time to help establish a routine. If we happen to miss one day, it's critical that we don't miss a second. Research also suggests that writing a plan that states exactly where and when we'll practise, as if we're making a contract with ourselves, significantly increases the chances of fulfilling it.

➢ *Congratulate ourselves* when we think our constructive thoughts and cope better with challenging situations. We could even give ourselves a treat to enhance our sense of achievement in these circumstances. Importantly, this will act to strengthen the reward component of the habit loop. While it may seem like a small thing to think our new thoughts, it represents a positive break from the past which deserves a reward.

➢ *Tell other people* we're close to about our harmful thoughts, how they are affecting us and what we're doing to improve our situation. This should help us persevere as the more people we inform and reach out to, the more questions we're likely to face regarding our progress, making it more difficult to give up! It's much easier to tell one person (ourselves) that we have 'failed' then ten people whose opinion we value.

➢ *Remind ourselves of the progress we're making* by comparing our current-selves with our past-selves. As I argued earlier, knowing that our efforts are making a difference will encourage us to carry on. If we struggle to remember how we used to feel we could refer to our original Thought Records or ask those who know us well. Keeping a diary that incorporates our thoughts and feelings is another way of achieving this.

➤ *Keep our objectives firmly in mind* as a further incentive to continue working. We should have a clear sense of our Target-Selves and how much better we'll feel when we get closer to it. If, rather than inspiring us, this simply emphasises how far we are from meeting our objectives, it's crucial to come up with obtainable, interim targets.

Building self-worth - Some dos and don'ts

Our aim here is to reach a point where we genuinely believe that we're valuable in our own right - that we have something to offer and what we do matters.

The 'correct' way of achieving this, or something much closer to it than we are now, is a matter of endless discussion and countless books. I have limited my contribution to some simple dos and don'ts that I think are vital and which I hope will provide some guidance.

Dos...

- Take charge

We must take responsibility for our self-worth as the first step to improving it. There's no point blaming other people's actions or bad luck for how we feel now and will likely feel in the future. This is not because they are blameless in all cases but because there's usually little we can do to change them or the situation (there are, of course, exceptions to this, particularly if we're suffering verbal or physical abuse).

We have the ability to determine what we think and, therefore, how we feel about ourselves. While we can't change the past, we can change the meaning we're giving to past events as well as choose how to interpret current and future situations. As Eleanor Roosevelt, former First Lady of the

United States, once famously said, '*No one can make you inferior without your consent.*' This is a very empowering message to keep in mind and one that lies at the heart of CBT as I described earlier.

- Exploit strengths and accept or work on weaknesses

Everyone has strengths and weaknesses. But one thing that separates the secure from the insecure is that the former are much better at accepting their weaknesses, not allowing them to dominate their lives, while making full use of their strengths. If we can replicate their success, then we too can reach a stronger, more secure place.

A useful starting point is to write down our strengths and weaknesses, generating a list of no more than three each (we can extend it later), with the number of strengths balancing the number of weaknesses. In forming the list, we should focus on different aspects of our personality. Below are some examples of what I mean.

Strengths	Weaknesses
Good sense of humour	Always worried about failing
Caring for others	Bad at socialising
Hardworking	Impatient with others

The best way of determining our strengths is to ask ourselves 'What would our best friend say are our strongest points?' and to derive our weaknesses 'What would our worst enemy say our weaknesses are?' I suspect that most of us will be better at coming up with the latter than the former and, if we struggle to identify strengths, then we may need to go ahead and actually ask our best friend (or family members) for help with this.

Having decided that our top two strengths are, say, a good sense of humour and a caring attitude then why not get involved in more situations where these characteristics will come to the fore? We could do some voluntary work if we have time and arrange with friends to go to the pub once a week, for example. By enjoying and appreciating our strengths more often we'll feel better about ourselves. It is, of course, important not to become boastful about them.

As for dealing with our weaknesses, we need to decide which ones, if any, we want to work on improving and which ones we will accept. For those we decide to tackle, we should devise a plan of action, while for those we opt to accept we must purposefully come to terms with them rather than hoping that they will go away - they won't! If this approach sounds familiar then that's because I wrote about Action Plans and Constructive Acceptance in chapter 7, meaning that we already have the necessary tools to make progress here.

Continuing with my example, let's say we choose to tackle our fear of failure. Just as before, we write a Thought Record as soon as possible after a relevant harmful thought has been triggered. We ask ourselves several questions designed to test the validity of that thought which, in turn, will help us derive some constructive alternatives. I have shown what our Record could look like overleaf.

Subsequently, every time we worry about failing, we call upon our constructive thoughts as well as using the behavioural techniques we find most helpful. We'll also implement the various methods we've learned to turn our new thoughts into habits. This, then, is our Action Plan.

	Thought Record - Fear of Failure
What was the trigger?	Upcoming exams
What did I think & how did I feel?	I was really worried about doing badly, letting myself and my family down. I thought I wouldn't be able to get a job
Is my thinking valid?	How have I done in past exams? Am I revising effectively? By thinking about the outcome of the exams will I improve my chances of doing well? Will my family still love me if I do badly?
What are some alternative, constructive thoughts?	*I've done okay in the past and can do so again* *My hard work will see me through* *I'll try my best and see where that gets me* *I'll focus on achieving my revision plan*

Meanwhile, we might decide to Constructively Accept that we're not particularly good at socialising. The best way of doing this is to come up with thoughts such as 'It doesn't matter if there's a short pause in a two-way conversation. I don't always have to be the one that thinks of the next thing to say,' 'I may not be great at small talk but I'm still worth talking to' or 'I'm not the only one who feels uncomfortable in social situations. Millions do.'

Constructively Accepting that we're bad at something is simply acknowledging that we're just like *everybody* else in the world - imperfect.

- Decide upon and defend core values

Given that we're no longer letting our weaknesses define us, what will take their place? Together with our strengths, it should be our core values and beliefs - the things that are really important to us, that we won't compromise on and which we're prepared to defend to the hilt. They could be religious beliefs or character traits such as loyalty, open-mindedness, humility, perseverance, compassion and putting others first. Our strengths may help us identify our core values as the two are likely to be closely linked.

The only core value I suggest that we should *all* have is a belief in ourselves - the sense that we can achieve our (realistic) targets, that we have the tools to deal effectively with difficult and anxious situations and that we can come back successfully from mistakes and failures. Corny I know, but vital and perfectly attainable by using the techniques described in this book.

One thing that should *not* define us is what we do for a living or indeed anything that could prove temporary. By choosing something ephemeral we run the risk of losing a large part of our identity at the drop of a hat and often through no fault of our own. If we ask ourselves 'Who am I?' our answer should be caring, reliable, truthful or motivated, for example, rather than accountant, nurse or postman.

Holding on to our values will help guide us through life, often directing our decisions when faced with difficult choices. It will also ensure that we're not a 'yes-man', agreeing to anything requested of us for the sake of a quiet life. Such individuals are usually taken for granted and fail to gain much, if any, respect.

With this in mind, we need to come up with a short list, itemising our red lines - what it is that we'll stick to and live by. It's important to recognise that these are *our* values and other people may well have very different ones. We cannot and should not try to impose our beliefs on them but accept and respect the differences between us. Where there is doubt, try to give other people the benefit of it. In our increasingly multicultural societies this is more important than ever.

- Live with purpose

As well as gaining a better understanding of who we are - our strengths, weaknesses and core values - we should also have a good idea of what it is we want to achieve in the future. While 'living in the moment' can be very helpful in certain situations, particularly as a means to overcome anxiety, we do need to look ahead at times, setting goals for ourselves. In the absence of such objectives it's very easy to drift, letting the weeks, months and years pass by without gaining any sense of accomplishment. American Major League Baseball player Jackie Robinson put it as follows...

'Life is not a spectator sport. If you're going to spend your whole life in the grandstand just watching what goes on, in my opinion you're wasting your life.'

When discussing the importance of goals with somebody I met on holiday many years ago, I was struck by his strongly held view that they were a bad thing and, to the extent that he had one himself, it was *'Not to have goals!'* To my mind, the main problem with this is that it conflicts with the way we're built. It's in our nature to seek improvement and not to do so will leave most of us feeling a lack of purpose and generally unsatisfied with life.

If we don't have any clear aims at present (other than getting closer to becoming our Target-Selves of course!) then our first goal should be to come up with one or two! They don't always have to involve 'helping others' or 'giving back' and they can be lifelong goals and/or shorter-term ones that we replace now and again. As long as they're worthwhile and achievable they'll provide a valuable sense of purpose to our lives.

It's also helpful to make a point of accomplishing something *every* day. We shouldn't go to sleep feeling that our waking hours have been worthless, particularly if we've had a bad day. Going for a walk, writing a catch-up email or learning something, is far better than nothing.

- Laugh at life

We can afford to take most situations far less seriously than we currently do. The majority of us are lucky enough not to worry about where our next meal is coming from, if we'll find shelter for the night and be warm enough to survive it, whether we'll be attacked or have to attack and where we can receive medical attention if needs be. Imagine what our long lost forebears would say if they could witness the mental trials and tribulations we put ourselves through. I don't suppose they would be all that sympathetic!

As I suggested previously, we have an unhelpful tendency of turning largely trivial situations into matters of near life and death. Although, ironically, this is part of what we inherited from our forebears, we're sophisticated enough to overcome it, both in the ways I described in chapter 8 as well as laughing at ourselves more often. 'So what if I make a mistake or fail at something?' 'Is it that important if he likes me or not?' 'Who cares if she is better than me at this?' At present, most of us carry burdens that are figments of our imagination and which can be relieved by taking a different perspective. Choose to be more happy-go-lucky and see what happens; err on the side of optimism when uncertain about something or somebody.

No doubt this will elicit responses such as 'What's the point? We'll just end up being disappointed.' My answer is that we can sometimes alter the outcome of a situation by adopting an alternative outlook. If we approach somebody who we fear will be difficult, then they are more likely to be difficult than if we approach them with positive body language. If we think we will fail at something, we're more likely to fail than if we believe we will succeed. If we do happen to be wrong, then we now have the techniques to deal with the disappointment.

...and don'ts

- Don't treat yourself as you would your worst enemy but your best friend

Something many of us do is treat ourselves as we would our worst enemy, beating ourselves up mentally and even physically sometimes. But why? Often, it's because the expectations we have of ourselves are unrealistically high as a result of past, inappropriate comparisons.

A large part of what I have written so far concerns how to change the way we think in these circumstances and I won't repeat myself here. There is one more thing we can do, however - start thinking about ourselves as we do our best friend. If he gets something wrong or makes a mistake, we don't think any less of him but help put things in perspective for him; if he feels inferior to somebody, we don't abuse him verbally or physically but tell him that he has other strengths; if he's always trying to prove himself to others we're not unpleasant to him, but point out that we like him for who he is.

I accept that we can go too far here, excusing ourselves when we need to learn from a situation or blaming others when we should be taking responsibility. But given where most of us are coming from, I think it's unlikely that this will happen often, at least for the time being. If and when it does, we should have sufficient control of our thoughts to take the necessary action.

- Don't be cowardly but courageous

There are and will continue to be times when we're desperate to avoid challenging situations; to run away and pretend we're not involved, only confronting them half-heartedly if we have no other option. By so doing, we won't have to test ourselves, confront our weaknesses or deal with our demons. If we fail, than we have a ready-made excuse - 'I wasn't really trying.'

Usually, however, the easy option is not the right one - another cliché for which I apologise! By summoning the courage to do something we would rather not, we will achieve and experience more, to the likely benefit of our self-worth. Even if this is not the outcome, taking the simple route doesn't always turn out as we expect it to. The more we delay, the bigger the obstacle will become, at least mentally, potentially reaching seemingly insurmountable proportions. Avoidance could also see us losing the respect of others and, more importantly, the respect of ourselves.

We should keep in mind that the only way of increasing our comfort zone is to move outside it. As we get older, we tend to forget that this is exactly how we developed as children - experimenting without the fear of failure, learning the lessons and moving on to the next stage. To achieve it as adults will often involve us consciously summoning the courage to act. When we do so, more often than not we'll discover that the most difficult step was the first one rather that what followed from taking it.

- Don't try to be somebody other than yourself

Our self-worth has to be built on how we feel about ourselves, not what we might feel if it were possible to be somebody else.

As we progress through life, we come across individuals or specific characteristics in people that we would like to copy. But while we can and should learn from those we admire, we mustn't try to be somebody other than our selves. If we do, we're setting ourselves up to fail as it's impossible to seamlessly adopt another person's characteristic(s), let alone their whole identity. We could, for example, choose to take tips from somebody we find amusing, such as laughing at our idiosyncrasies. We shouldn't attempt to tell the same jokes in the same manner, however. If we do, we'll come across as fake.

Even if it was possible to perfectly replicate aspects of other people, it's completely unnecessary to do so. There's enough within all of us that is interesting, unusual, quirky or amusing without having to take on board somebody else's persona: we should focus on what we have and could develop rather than what we don't. If it doesn't seem like that, then we need to search harder within ourselves to discover and appreciate these features. If we think that others can't see it, we should be aware that this may simply reflect a misperception on our part or, for whatever reason, that they're choosing not to look for it. Perhaps because they are a little insecure themselves, many people talk endlessly about their achievements and experiences, rather than enquiring about ours, turning what should be a conversation into a monologue. Determine not to be one of those people.

- Don't think of others as competitors but allies (generally)

Every year the UN publishes the "World Happiness Report", which, amongst other things, ranks 159 countries according to their level of 'happiness'. Intriguingly, the Nordic countries always perform extremely well - the latest results for 2019 placing Finland, Denmark, Norway and Iceland (in that order) at the top of the tree, while Sweden was seventh. For the record, the UK came fifteenth and the US nineteenth.

When questioned about the reasons for this, the head of the Happiness Research Institute, Meik Wiking, suggested the nature of these Social Democratic States meant that there was '*less to compete for...less incentive to be cut throat*' than in the US or UK for example. Rather than happiness being seen as a '*zero sum game*' there was more of a sense that, '*my happiness also depends on others' happiness*.'

A similar argument was made by Siobhan Robbins of Sky News when writing about a rumoured royal feud in the UK between Kate and Meghan in December 2018...

'*The unceasing undermining and criticism of the Duchesses feeds a cultural trend where women are constantly compared and competing. Every aspect is judged and ranked. Two women can't be different...one has to be better. It works to divide and corrode the unbeatable power and happiness a female support network can provide.*'

Both quotes emphasise the importance of trying to see other people as allies not competitors - part of the same team, rather than someone we have to beat. Achieving this will often require a mindset change, which, if we can deliver, will put us at greater ease, supporting the work we're doing to relieve the sense of threat that so often accompanies our comparisons.

Of course, there will be times, such as during sporting competition, when other people *are* competitors and should be thought of as such. When making comparisons in these contexts we should focus on what we can learn from the opposition and how we're going to adjust our game-plan, rather than feeling intimidated or overconfident. At the same time, we mustn't forget about our own strengths - what we do well. I will look in greater detail at the various strategies we can use when (legitimately) competing in chapter 15.

In brief

Turning our new constructive thoughts into habits as speedily as possible makes it more likely that they'll dominate our old, destructive ways of thinking. Among other things, this can be achieved by strengthening the reward component of the habit loop as well as mentally rehearsing them as part of a daily routine.

Building a genuine, lasting sense of self-worth is also critical to staying the course, particularly now that we're no longer relying on downward comparisons to do the heavy lifting. Rather than have our perceived weaknesses drive our life's course, it should be our strengths and core values that do so. We must locate them and bring them to the fore. Living with purpose and laughing at life will also help, as will adopting a more courageous approach to challenging situations. We should also try hard to think about ourselves and others as allies not enemies.

Chapter 10

Part 1, Summary

I have covered a lot of ground over the last nine chapters, discussing the problems social comparisons can create for our mental health and how we can take control to make them work to our benefit instead. Before moving on let's remind ourselves of the main points.

➤ How we perceive ourselves is heavily affected by the comparisons we make with others as well as those they make with us. We're all products of our comparisons.

➤ There's a large chunk of luck whether the targets for our comparisons are appropriate given that we typically choose the most convenient individuals to compare ourselves with. If they're unsuitable and we believe the results of the comparisons, which we're prone to do, we can arrive at a highly inaccurate impression of ourselves.

➤ Even accurate impressions of where we stand relative to appropriate others may have undesirable effects depending on how we react to the results.

➤ Academic research confirms that comparisons can create problems for our psychological well-being, with issues of inferiority and/or superiority most commonly cited. The damaging feelings we experience are created by thoughts that are automatically triggered when we encounter particular situations.

➢ The advent and extraordinary growth of social media has dramatically altered the nature and number of comparisons we make. There's growing evidence that intensive use of many of these platforms is having detrimental effects on the mental health of young people in particular.

➢ To remedy the harmful influences of our comparisons and turn them to our advantage we must adjust our thinking. Using Thought Records and plenty of practise we need to invalidate our current negative thoughts, replacing them with constructive alternatives. If our current thoughts can't be disproved then we have a choice - Constructively Accept the situation or come up with an Action Plan to improve it. Similar methods will help us deal with mistakes and failures.

➢ Ultimately, we're aiming to achieve three things. First, to be resilient to upward comparisons that will represent a genuine source of motivation and learning. Second, to no longer rely on downward comparisons to inflate our ego. And third, to make comparisons with our past and Target-Selves purely to monitor progress and remind ourselves of where we're heading.

➢ There are a large number of behavioural techniques we can use to reinforce our cognitive actions and increase the probability of success. These include Exposure Therapy, composure techniques and problem sharing.

➤ To help stay the course we should also work on turning our new thoughts and behaviours into habits as well as strengthening our sense of self-worth. There are several dos and don'ts when it comes to building a greater sense of security. It's particularly important to be clear about our core values and relative strengths as they, rather than our weaknesses and failures, are what should define us from now on.

➤ Using these various tools we'll be able to transform the nature of our comparisons and how we react to them. Many positive developments should follow. Instead of feeling threatened by other people and competitive environments, we'll see them as potential sources of fun, learning or motivation; the same will be true of how we respond to losses and failures, while we'll also be better able to enjoy our successes as well as those of people we care for; we won't feel the same need to put others down or prove ourselves; we'll be more resilient to criticism and less concerned about what others may or may not think of us. In short, we'll be stronger, healthier and happier.

PART 2

COMPARISONS IN 'EXTERNAL' SITUATIONS

Chapter 11

Seeking Comparative Advantage

Claims and aims

Our comparisons don't just influence the perception we have of ourselves, but virtually everything and everybody around us. If you don't believe me, try watching a game of children's football refereed by an adult - the chances are that you'll end up convinced that the referee is huge...until you stand next to him or her! Perhaps you have bought a TV that looks a perfectly reasonable size in the shop only to realise that it's enormous when you get it home? Maybe you have returned to your old school for the first time since leaving it several years previously to find that everything has shrunk or marvelled at how small a pool table is when you're used to playing snooker on a full-sized version.

As we discovered in the first part of the book, the effects of comparisons on our inner-self can be helpful or unhelpful and need to be managed carefully. We often have to change the comparisons we make and/or the meaning we attach to them to progress. The same is true of how we use comparisons to assess things other than ourselves and make decisions about them. Building on some of the lessons of part 1, the aim here is to learn how to maximise the advantages and minimise the disadvantages of comparisons in 'external' situations.

Living with comparisons

I will focus on five wide-ranging situations, many of which we encounter daily and all of which can have profound implications for us.

1. **Living.** The quantity and nature of food we consume is affected by a range of comparisons, including how much those sitting around the dinner table with us partake of. Changing our comparisons can help us achieve our weight related aims. Our comparisons also effect how fast we drive and how aggressive we are on the roads. Meanwhile, the popularity of online dating sites has stimulated comparisons in an area where they didn't exist so extensively before. The inferences are fascinating.

2. **Buying.** When deciding what to purchase we usually compare a range of competing products or services. Retailers are very well aware of this and, by using a variety of tactics, attempt to influence the results we reach. While we may *believe* that we're in full control of what we buy and how much we're prepared to pay for it, this is more the exception than the rule. The good news is that it's possible to gain greater sway.

3. **Working.** The use of appropriate comparisons can be extremely potent when persuading colleagues and clients to come round to our way of thinking. At the same time, key decisions at work - including who to hire and fire, which staff deserve the best bonuses and whether to change jobs - frequently see us *misuse* comparisons with significant repercussions. I consider what we can do in response and whether Artificial Intelligence systems will help or hinder.

4. **Sporting.** Comparisons are a huge part of competitive games and sport with the power to either improve or reduce our chances of winning. They're also important for those of us watching from the sidelines, often leading us to make misjudgments with painful consequences for our credibility and wallets. We can learn to avoid common mistakes and use comparisons to our competitive advantage.

5. **Investing.** Comparisons frequently lead us into all sorts of trouble when it comes to investing our savings. Seeing others 'get rich' pressurises us to buy when we shouldn't, while our greater fear of losing money than our joy of gaining it means that we take less risk than we sometimes should. We also postpone investment decisions, wrongly expecting the future to offer greater clarity than the past and assess the quality of our past investments inappropriately.

For each of these situations, I investigate the sort of comparisons we make, how they influence the decisions we reach and, where relevant, what we can do to improve them. In many instances, simply achieving a better understanding of the potential pitfalls of our existing comparisons will help us avoid repeating the same costly mistakes. But there are also ways in which we can use comparisons to gain an edge.

Chapter 12

Living

Our day to day living - how much we eat and drink, the way we drive, who we date, the DIY we do and so on - is affected by the comparisons we make. Being aware of the role played by these comparisons will improve the quality of our decisions in these situations.

Weight control

Medical practitioners argue that the best way of obtaining and sustaining an appropriate weight is to *'develop healthy eating habits that suit our personal lifestyle.'* This is far more easily suggested than achieved. A survey by Mintel in 2016 found that 64% of UK adults attempt to shed weight *'all or most of the time'*, generally jumping on and falling off specific dieting programmes of various varieties. Our comparisons are a double-edged sword when it comes to our eating and drinking behaviours, having the potential to help us with our weight related ambitions, but throwing us off course if we're not careful.

A mistake we commonly make here is to confuse concepts of relative and absolute - *healthier* eating and drinking habits don't always equate to *healthy* ones. For instance, while halving our consumption of chips from two portions a day to one represents an improvement, it's still far from ideal. Similarly, we may share a dinner table with people who eat a single portion of fruit and vegetables every day and conclude that by eating two such portions we have a good diet. In truth, we just have a slightly better one than they do.

Manufacturers and retailers don't always help us in this regard either. True, in most advanced countries, claims (or even hints) that products are 'low' in fat, sugar or calories can now only be made if they contain less than a certain amount of these things - which, in the EU, is 3g, 5g and 40kcal respectively per 100g. But there are a couple of other tricks to look out for. First, a low *fat* item doesn't necessarily mean that it's low in *calories* because sugar is often used to replace fat. Second, companies can still advertise their products as '*lower* in fat' or having '*reduced* calories', which many of us interpret as low fat or low calorie. They are also permitted to point out that their product has '*less* fat/sugar/calories' than comparable items, potentially leading us to the same conclusion.

At the time of writing, the helpful traffic-light food-labelling system - clearly indicating whether items contain 'low', 'medium' or 'high' levels of fat, saturated fat, sugar and salt by using the colours green, amber and red - is only voluntary in the UK. Most supermarkets support it, although a significant number of manufacturers still don't use it.

Another issue to be wary of is using inappropriate comparisons to reach conclusions about our weight and body shape - 'I'm lighter than my sister, therefore I'm light' or 'I must be eating too much as my classmate is a size 8 and I'm a size 10' are examples of this. They may seem crazy in the cold light of day, but the fact is that many of us use them to justify how much or how little we eat and drink.

In each of the situations I've described, it's up to us to recognise the mistakes we're making and change the way we compare. Rather than comparing our weight and what we eat and drink to friends, family or models, we should be aware of how we measure up to the appropriate weight for somebody of our gender and physical stature as well as what constitutes a healthy diet. Having done this, we'll be much better placed to know whether we're regularly consuming too many unhealthy things and are above or below a healthy weight.

If we subsequently decide to adjust our eating and drinking habits there are several ways we can use comparisons to our advantage. Assuming that we're trying to shed weight, classic examples include eating from relatively small plates and drinking from modestly sized glasses. The aim here is to convince ourselves that we're consuming more than we really are. The opposite applies if we're attempting to gain weight.

Buffets can be a big challenge if we're aiming to be lighter. Although we're often provided with absurdly small plates in these circumstances, the temptation to pile them high and return to the counter several times 'to get our money's worth' is often too much to resist. I know it is for me! We should be wary of buying large packets of crisps or big tubs of ice cream as well. Although it may be cheaper to do so, those of us with limited self-control will end up eating more than we otherwise would and should. In Economics, 'Says Law' states that, 'Supply creates its own demand' and this is also highly pertinent when it comes to how much we consume: the more food and drink that's readily available, the more we're likely to partake of.

When we're eating and drinking it's incredibly easy to add calories without really thinking about it - 'I'll have an extra scoop of ice cream,' 'A can of fizzy drink would be nice with my meal' or 'Just one more pint of lager' are good examples of this. Even knowing the calories involved in consuming these items probably won't make a great deal of difference - '180 calories for a packet of crisps is not much is it?' But what if we were compare the calories of 'unhealthy' items with something else to generate greater meaning? This could be our Recommended Daily Amount (RDA) of calories or the amount of exercise we would need to complete to burn off the additional calories.

I have made these comparisons for a number of different 'add-on' foods and drinks in the table below, using walking as the exercise (it could, of course, be running, cycling or whatever is most relevant to you).

Food & Drink	Calories (kcal, approx)	% of RDA* Women, Men	Walking Equivalent** Women, Men
35g packet of crisps	184	9%, 7%	2.2, 1.8 miles
35g of dry-roasted peanuts	205	10%, 8%	2.4, 2.1 miles
Cheese sandwich	261	13%, 10%	3.1, 2.6 miles
100g of chocolate ice cream	216	11%, 9%	2.6, 2.2 miles
2 shortbread biscuits	180	9%, 7%	2.1, 1.8 miles
Pint of lager	160	8%, 6%	1.9, 1.6 miles
Pint of cider	200	10%, 8%	2.4, 2.0 miles
175ml glass of dry white wine	120	6%, 5%	1.4, 1.2 miles
300ml glass of orange juice	135	7%, 5%	1.6, 1.4 miles
330ml can of Coke/Pepsi	140-150	7%, 6%	1.7, 1.5 miles
270ml Mocha Frappuccino	180	9%, 7%	2.1, 1.8 miles

*Recommended Daily Amount, based on 2,000 calories for women & 2,500 for men. Numbers rounded to nearest percentage point
**Assumes a UK average weight - 70kg for women & 84kg for men

They put quite a different perspective on things. For example, a man who has drunk three pints of cider and eaten a packet of peanuts will have consumed nearly a third of his RDA and would need to walk about eight miles at a reasonable pace to work it off. A couple of cans of full sugar Pepsi and a regular packet of crisps consumed by a woman is equivalent to a quarter of her recommended calories and roughly five and a half miles of walking.

We'll probably think twice about eating or drinking these sorts of items by making these kind of comparisons.

There's a risk that you might consider me a member of the 'fun police' in this context, although I promise you I'm not! I enjoy snacks and drinks as much as the next person (probably more) and am not suggesting we avoid them completely.

Driving

The decisions we make when driving can obviously have profound implications both for ourselves and other road users, meaning that anything we can do to improve them should be seized upon. There are numerous ways in which comparisons play a role here, and I have described some of the most important below. As you will see, mistakes are common and our aim should be to avoid repeating them while being more understanding of those who do.

Journey times

When driving on a motorway have you ever found yourself thinking that you could save a lot of time by speeding up to 80mph from your current 70mph? Or perhaps you've been travelling at 70mph and see somebody zooming past you at a ridiculous speed, presumably attempting to do the same thing. If so, you or they are likely to be experiencing a 'Time Saving Bias!'

Let's say we have *50 miles* left on our journey and instead of staying at 70mph we decide to increase it to 80mph because we're running late. How much time will we save? The answer is less than five and a half minutes. If you don't believe me have a look at the calculations below, comparing how long it will take to drive the 50 miles at the different speeds.

50 miles @ 70mph = (50m÷70mph)*60mins = 42.9 minutes
50 miles @ 80mph = (50m÷80mph)*60mins = 37.5 minutes

But what if, instead, we were travelling at 30 mph and were able to up it to 40 mph for the remaining 50 miles of our trip? We would save an impressive 25 minutes, probably more than we would anticipate.

50 miles @ 30mph = (50m÷30mph)*60mins = 100 minutes
50 miles @ 40mph = (50m÷40mph)*60mins = 75 minutes

Our tendency to overestimate the time we save by increasing our speed from a relatively high level and underestimate it when raising our speed from a comparatively low level has been revealed in several different studies. The relationship between our driving speed and journey time is *not* linear, contrary to our implicit assumptions.

So, when we're already driving quickly and find ourselves tempted to go even faster, we should consider whether the risk is worth the surprisingly small amount of time we'll save.

Speed perception

We're notoriously bad at judging the speed of moving vehicles, not least the one we're driving. That's why we have speedometers to guide us. The trouble is the more time we spend looking at the dial the less time we'll have to scrutinise the road. As a result, we're forced to make frequent judgements about the speed we're travelling at which are very easy to get wrong and significantly so in certain circumstances.

When we have spent a long time driving on a motorway at 70mph (or, dare I say it, 80mph), 40mph is going to seem very sluggish: far slower than if we had previously been travelling at 20mph. Put another way, our internal speedometer is likely to suggest that we're going much slower than we actually are having departed a 'speedy' road and considerably faster in the case of a 'slower' road.

Even when looking down at a speedometer we can be fooled, depending on how it's configured. Have a glance at the pictures below, just as you would if driving a car, and determine which of the two is indicating the faster speed. Most people will guess the right hand one, whereas it's not. This is an extreme example but it illustrates the point, which is particularly pertinent when we drive an unfamiliar car with a different speedometer to the one we're used to.

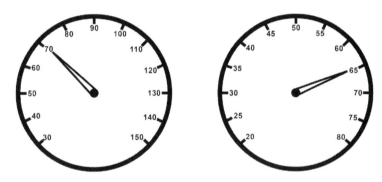

By selecting the 'correct' gear in a manual vehicle - in most cars it's difficult to ignore the sound of the engine when exceeding 50mph in third gear and 30mph in second gear, effectively forcing ourselves to drive within these speeds - we can reduce the chance of making some of these errors. If it's available in the car we're driving and safe to do so, we could also set cruise control to the appropriate speed.

So you think you're a better than average driver?

In Western societies at least, surveys have consistently found that the vast majority of us (typically around 80-90%) believe that we're better than average drivers! Indeed a US study conducted by a car insurance company, showed that even when using their phone to text or email, a remarkable 80% of people still thought they were an 'average' or 'above average' driver (44% and 36% respectively). 43% of men believed they were above average and 29% of women.

This effect, often dubbed 'Illusory Superiority' or the 'Dunning-Kruger Effect' has been found to exist in many different areas - including perceived teaching ability, memory, leadership and social skills - but has potentially dangerous consequences when it comes to driving. *If* it's true, we're likely to feel overconfident, blind to our ineptitude, and could be more prone to accidents as a result.

But do we *genuinely* believe that we're superior drivers and behave on the roads as such or are our answers a form of self-protection - a way of boosting our ego? It's interesting that the effect is more prevalent in areas that are vaguely defined, including driving, rather than in more specific fields where it's easier to be found out, such as tennis or chess. Another intriguing discovery is that people generally think that they are better than average at simple tasks and worse than average at difficult ones. To test this out...

Give yourself a rating between 0-10 (where 5 is average and 10 is the highest) of your bicycle riding abilities

Give yourself a rating between 0-10 (where 5 is average and 10 is the highest) of your unicycle riding abilities

The chances are you will award yourself a higher score for bicycle riding than unicycle riding and you may well be right.

However, far more than 50% of people will probably do the same - the *actual* average of responses will be more than 5 in the first case and less than 5 in the second. Attempting to explain this phenomenon, Don Moore from Carnegie Mellon University, has suggested that even when we're explicitly asked to compare ourselves with others, we often focus on the absolute rather than the relative[1] - 'I'm good at riding a bike...therefore I'm likely to be better than average.' 'I'm (probably) not good at riding a unicycle...therefore I must be worse than average.' In effect, we don't really compare at all, presumably because it's tricky to do so.

One possible implication of this is that the reason we think that we're better than average drivers is because we consider driving to be easy. But if we think driving is easy are we more or less likely to make mistakes?

Laying the blame

When *we* make a driving mistake (or other blunders for that matter) it's strange how it's almost always the fault of our situation - a passenger was distracting us, our line of vision was obstructed, there was something wrong with the car etc. But when *others* err it's generally a reflection of their carelessness, ability or who they are! In other words, our reaction is very different depending on who's made the mistake. Psychologists have a term for this - 'Fundamental Attribution Error' - and for the sake of our blood pressure as well as harmony on the roads it's important to be aware of it.

Apart from our natural inclination to want to shift the blame, the difference in approach stems from the fact that we have more information about our situation compared with that of our fellow road users. Because we're likely to be ignorant of the external factors that may have caused another driver to miscalculate we look for the easy answer instead - 'It must be because they're stupid!'

With this in mind, the next time somebody makes a mistake, try not to rush to judgement: consider the (distinct) possibility that it has a situational explanation. After all, if it's good enough to justify many of our gaffes then it *should* be good enough to legitimise other peoples errors as well.

Aggressive driving

Numerous studies have investigated the characteristics of relatively aggressive drivers and the conditions associated with aggressive actions. One of the most extensive was an observational study in the US involving over 2,000 episodes of belligerent behaviour - including beeping of horns, cutting across one or more lanes in front of other vehicles and passing on the shoulders.[2] The results were what you might expect. Controlling for their relative numbers, men were more aggressive than women and those aged less than 45 more than those older than 45. Drivers who were alone in their vehicle were also slightly more aggressive than those who had passengers. Greater hostility was shown during rush hour, when the value of time is high, than at other periods of the day.

More interestingly, others studies have examined whether there is any relationship between aggressive acts on the roads and the *status* of either the aggressor or the target of the aggression. Some have found that, 'high status' individuals (as indicated by the value of their car) were more aggressive compared to 'low status' individuals, while low status 'frustrators' were subjected to a greater number of aggressive acts than high status ones. This is by no means a unanimous conclusion, however.

The reason may be that it's the *relative* status of the potential aggressor and frustrator that matters: a high status driver is more likely to be aggressive if he deems his frustrator to be of low status, while a low status driver will be more aggressive with high status frustrators. This fits with the conclusions of a University of Bern study[3] and seems sensible when bearing in mind what we know about 'in-group' biases - our tendency to be more cooperative with people who we deem to be similar to us.

Dating

In chapter 2, I pointed out how the comparisons we make with our partners can affect the quality of our relationships and hence our psychological well-being. Here, I'm interested in how our comparisons influence who we choose to date.

Dating decisions are traditionally very different to most of our decisions. To begin with, unlike buying a washing machine for instance, it involves a two-way process whereby both parties must agree to date for the date to happen - a washing machine obviously can't refuse to be bought! Also, we're not usually presented with a wide range of potential partners which we then compare to come to a decision. We might assess the similarities and differences between ourselves and our date as well as between our current date and those we've previously dated, but that's about as far as our comparisons are likely to extend.

As such, who we date appears to be one of the few areas in life where comparisons don't have a huge role to play: where the *absolute* - whether we're attracted to the person and they are attracted to us - genuinely matters more than the *relative* - how the individual measures up to everybody else who may or may not want to date us. Or is it?

Online platforms are rapidly transforming the dating landscape, as illustrated by the numbers below.

➢ There were around 8,000 dating sites in the world in 2018 (Forbes, reported in DatingNews.com).

➢ Nearly 50 million Americans have tried online dating at some point (Statistic Brain Institute reported in DatingNews.com).

➢ 19% of all US internet users accessed dating websites or apps in April 2017, of which 36% were using them daily and 80% had met someone in person through them (Statista).

➢ In 2015, nearly 60% of people thought online dating was a good way to meet potential dates (Pew Research Center, reported in DatingNews.com).

➢ Online dating is now the second most common way for heterosexual American couples to meet (the first is in a bar) and the most common for homosexual couples (Business Insider, October 2017).

➢ Recent surveys have reported that 20% of current relationships began online and 19% of couples who married within the last year met on a dating site (Statistic Brain Institute reported in DatingNews.com and the Knot).

➢ 84% of dating app users stated they were looking for a romantic relationship, as opposed to friendship (Statista).

There are now so many people using online dating sites that even if we restrict our search to a fairly narrow geographical area, we'll normally still be presented with hundreds, if not thousands, of potential partners. Assuming we're unwilling to contact every one of them, we'll have to whittle down the number in some other way. We generally do so by comparing the different individuals based on the information included in their 'profile', which may or may not be accurate. In a survey by eHarmony, a remarkable 53% of people *admitted* to lying on their dating profile, with men more likely to do so with regards to their income and women their age.

So what is the effect of using dating sites and hence comparisons on the quality of our dating decisions? The most rigorous analysis of the question to date, albeit one that was produced several years ago now, was not particularly positive.

In their 2012 paper,[4] Eli Finkel and colleagues argued that browsing profiles or making side-by-side comparisons leads us to prioritise different characteristics than when meeting potential partners face-to-face. Not surprisingly, physical appearance and income typically receive more attention than 'softer' qualities. The one-dimensional nature of profiles, which can't convey traits such a person's sense of humour, makes this all but inevitable and the result is that a relatively small number of individuals end up attracting the bulk of online attention. This leaves a lot of willing suitors dissatisfied and the targets of their affections often so overwhelmed by offers that they end up quitting the sites. Also, if and when we go on a date, we're often surprised by our failure to click with the other individual.

By encouraging us to make comparisons, online dating sites stimulate an assessment mindset where, according to the authors, we...

'...objectify potential partners, commoditizing them as options available in a marketplace of profiles. Perhaps more than in conventional offline dating, an online dater may immediately assess the likely rewards and costs associated with forming a relationship with a certain partner, relative to alternatives, and use these assessments to decide whether to pursue further contact.'

In other words, our decision making process becomes more akin (although still far from identical) to that of buying something like a washing machine. It gets worse, however. This evaluative way of thinking can spill over into our subsequent relationships. It's suggested that rather than being based on communality - sharing tasks with our partner and providing mutual support to each other - they are more likely to involve reciprocity - one person doing something on the assumption that the other will return the favour. The latter is widely considered to be bad news for the health and durability of relationships.

Another downside of the significant choice provided by online sites is the threat it poses to loyalty within the relationship. After all, we know that if things get tricky there's a huge number of potential alternative partners accessible at the press of a button and a short online message.

Given these choice related issues, one option is to change the way we compare, paying more attention to potential partners' interests and reported personality traits as well as ignoring those people that are likely to be 'out of our league'. At the same time, our own profile should of course be truthful (!) and, I suggest, focus on our core values - what's most important to us and we what we appreciate in others (see chapter 9).

We could also concentrate on those sites that narrow the field on our behalf through the use of 'matching algorithms'. It's important to note that underlying most of these rule-based systems is the view that opposites *don't* attract or at least generally don't end up in satisfying long-term relationships. As a result, we're normally paired with people who are similar to ourselves in important respects. The merits of this are hotly disputed but suffice to say there's little evidence that such sites yield better results than others, while some argue they may even be inferior.

In truth, there's no substitute to meeting face-to-face, implying that a date that is initiated offline is more likely to be successful (assuming we already know the person we've chosen to date) than an online date. The trouble is, unless we venture online, the chances are we won't be going on many dates!

Great British obsessions!

I couldn't finish this chapter without briefly mentioning how comparisons influence the way we think about three of the UK's national obsessions - the weather, Do-It-Yourself (DIY) and the National Lottery (now called Lotto).

The weather

The good thing about bad weather is that when we get some good weather we're likely to enjoy it more than if we hadn't had the bad weather in the first place...if you see what I mean! In other words, if the weather is always nice then the beneficial effect of an additional sunny day will soon become very small because we have nothing bad to compare it with. It's precisely why we should think very carefully about moving to sunnier climes *just* 'for the weather'.

Our expectations are also important here. We appreciate even a vaguely sunny day in winter not just because it's an improvement on what came before but because it's probably better than we were anticipating. If we experienced the same hours of sunshine and temperature as that good winter day in the middle of summer then we would probably be very disappointed for the opposite reason - it would be worse than our expectations.

Similarly, if we're promised an excellent day's weather by a reputable meteorologist and it doesn't materialise then this will seem worse than if we were blissfully unaware of the projection or the forecast was for inclement conditions. Perhaps this means that weather forecasts should always err on the side of pessimism (if they don't already) just as *we* should do if somebody asks us to predict the future. The adage of under-promising with the intention of over-delivering is a potent one precisely because we can't help but compare what has occurred with what we expected or were told would happen.

DIY

Although the rush to rent by mobile millennials is slightly undermining the UK's DIY fixation, the sound of hammering, sawing, drilling or cutting can still be heard in most streets on most weekends. In theory at least, DIY is also easier than ever now, with countless online videos and TV property shows available to help us solve any problem we might encounter as well as reveal the enviable results of home improvement enthusiasts 'just like us'.

A word of warning though. For those of us thinking about transforming parts of our property, we need to be aware that once we have done that (assuming our efforts are successful), we'll probably feel compelled to improve other parts of the house and garden as well. This isn't necessarily because we'll have been bitten by the DIY bug, but rather because when one thing looks better, our urge to compare means related objects immediately look worse. I'm sure you'll have noticed that a newly painted room makes the furniture within those four walls appear tattier, while other rooms will beg for your attention as well; new kitchen worktops will ensure that the cupboards above and below them suddenly need replacing; smarter wall tiles in the bathroom will make the floor tiles appear worse; laying new turf in the garden will mean that we feel pressure to tidy up the weed-infested borders and so on.

In some ways this comparison effect is advantageous and I'm certainly not advocating a DIY-less world. It will, however, mean that we'll end up spending more time, effort and money than we first anticipated as one improvement leads to pressure for another...and another.

The same phenomenon applies to other aspects of our lives as well. For example, if we buy a new suit, we may also have to purchase new shoes as our old ones no longer look acceptable; if we stay in an expensive hotel (and enjoy it), then subsequent, cheaper versions will seem worse than they otherwise would and if we watch *some* TV programmes in Ultra High Definition (UHD) then those that are not available in this format will appear to be of very low quality.

The National Lottery

It's reported that around 70% of UK adults, roughly 37 million people, 'regularly' play the lottery, with half of us doing so more than once a month. But why? We all know that we're incredibly unlikely to win, don't we?

A survey by the software company Vision Critical in the US, found that 75% of lottery participants believe that they *will* eventually win. Assuming a similar figure in the UK, this suggests that Lotto players are far more optimistic than they should be. Since it began in 1994 up until May 2018, roughly 5,100 people had walked away with at least £1million. This may sound like a lot but isn't when you consider how many millions of us participated during those 24 years. Even the 38,691 individuals that won at least £50,000 should consider themselves extraordinarily fortunate compared to the rest of us.

We generally make two mistakes. First, we believe that we're far luckier than the average person - a non sequitur but, as we've discovered, perfectly plausible! Second, we're very bad at conceptualising large numbers. According to Lotto we usually have about a one in 45 million chance of scooping the jackpot if we buy a single ticket. We'll all recognise that represents a small probability but it's quite difficult to get our heads around quite how tiny it really is. Let me put it differently therefore. Imagine that you're sitting in a packed Wembley

Stadium (capacity 90,000) and there will be a solitary individual picked at random to win a prize. You probably wouldn't fancy your chances too much. Now imagine sitting in the same stadium and having 499 other Wembley stadiums packed to the rafters with fellow participants all with the same probability as you of winning. I hope you're wearing your lucky pants!

The good news is that plenty of the money we use to play the lottery goes to worthwhile causes, meaning we could choose to see it as a form of charitable giving. If not, it represents a tax on those of us who are not very good at probability!

In brief

Understanding comparison effects will help improve many aspects of our everyday lives.

We can use comparisons much better than we do when it comes to our eating and drinking habits as well as judging our body shapes and the amount of exercise we undertake. There's a crucial distinction to be made between what is 'healthy' and what is 'healthier'. The latter is often confused with the former to justify something that is still far from ideal.

We also need to be more aware of comparison related driving mistakes. Picking up speed when we're already travelling quickly won't save much time; other peoples' driving errors have the same causes as our own; our perceived superiority is often illusory; and status differences are, but needn't be, responsible for many aggressive acts on the roads.

Online dating is not just revolutionising the way we find potential partners. Research suggests that by encouraging a comparison mindset the implications for the quality of ensuing relationships could be profound.

Chapter 13

Buying

The role of comparisons

How do we reach a decision to buy a particular product or service? The process typically involves four steps...

First, we establish the need or desire to purchase something. Often this stems from *comparisons* we make with other people. 'My brother has a nice watch. I want to get one as well,' 'I'd like a cool haircut similar to my friend' or 'I've seen somebody on social media who looks great in that jacket. I think I'll buy it.'

Second, we search for the product, meaning that we visit a physical store which is likely to stock it and/or look online.

Third, we're generally faced with a choice, leading us to *compare* various options of the same or similar product (unless we already know what we're going to buy as a result of previous comparisons or are loyal to a particular brand). We'll *compare* prices as well as other characteristics such as the functionality, practicality and 'look and feel' of the various possibilities. We might also *compare* customer reviews - what is the overall rating of the different options, what do people like and dislike about them?

Finally, with all this information in mind, we come to a decision, choosing which of the items to purchase or opting to 'walk away'.

Clearly, comparisons are fundamental to our shopping experience. Without them, it would be difficult to know if we're getting value for money, while they also open our eyes to different possibilities and inspire us to search for particular items.

Retailers are very much aware of the sort of comparisons we make and, not surprisingly, attempt to influence the decisions we reach. They do this in the knowledge that our inherent laziness and/or lack of time mean that we're usually reluctant to undertake extensive research as well as being receptive to shortcuts that simplify our decision making. This can be true even when it comes to our biggest purchases. We're often perfectly willing to part with several thousands of pounds to buy a car or hundreds of thousands to purchase a house based on minimal investigation.

At the same time, however, retailers generally face intense competition when selling their products. This can work to our advantage, although it also incentivises them to find distinctive and cunning ways to 'manage' our comparisons...within the confines of the relevant laws of course!

Another element affecting the nature of our comparisons and the balance of power between retailers and consumers is the changing way in which we shop. Recent surveys indicate that more than 50% of people in the US and UK now prefer to buy online, with roughly 80% having already made an online purchase of some variety at some point. The latter compares with little more than 20% in the early noughties. Although it's tempting to assume that the rapid growth of e-commerce (and now mobile commerce – m-commerce) has made it practically impossible for retailers to manipulate our comparisons, it's fair to say that many of them have adapted successfully to the new environment!

In short, what we buy, where we buy it and what price we pay for it involves a complicated two-way process - we, as consumers, influence how retailers behave, while retailers influence the decisions we arrive at.

Inevitably, winners and losers (amongst both buyers and sellers) emerge from this and it's very easy to end up on the wrong side if we're not careful. The question is how can we make better decisions without it costing too much of our precious time?

Strategies, traps & solutions

A large part of the solution is to be more aware of the various strategies adopted by retailers, taking advantage of the benefits they yield while avoiding the traps set for the unsuspecting. The tactics used generally fall into two categories - deliberately undercutting the competition in terms of price and, more subtly, messing with our comparisons in numerous ways.

Undercutting the competition

Retailers' most obvious nudge to consumers is through the prices they set for the products they sell. One retailer attempting to boost their sales, could choose to undercut the competition, knowing that this will attract the attention of those shoppers that include them in their price comparison. This, of course, represents the whole ethos of some stores, such as 'Pound Shops' or 'Discount Supermarkets', while many others use this tactic temporarily.

As consumers confronting a relatively low price for a product, we need to be satisfied that the retailer hasn't compromised too much on quality for our liking. Retailers in the value space will attempt to convince us that they haven't with various tag lines. But some of us require more persuading than others, depending on our budgets, the time we're willing to spend researching the market and how inherently suspicious we are.

Patently, there is some truth behind the expression 'You get what you pay for', implying that a degree of scepticism is usually warranted when we're confronted with a relatively low price. It's also perfectly possible to be too wary, however. There are many reasons, other than poor quality, why retailers price something comparatively cheaply. It could be that their costs are relatively low, they are more efficient, they operate a 'stack it high, sell it cheap' strategy, they are selling a 'loss-leader' or simply want to clear their shelves of a particular item to restock them with something new.

Hence, those of us that can afford to buy more expensive items but still care about how much money we spend shouldn't automatically rule out low priced options - as strange as it may seem, many do! Give discount stores a chance at least. We might be surprised by what we find and if we decide that the quality is too low then we haven't exactly lost a great deal. Also, don't conclude that there's no such thing as a bargain, they do exist and others will snap them up if we're too sceptical to do so ourselves.

Messing with our price comparisons

If a retailer is unable or unwilling to charge the lowest price, there are plenty of other tactics they can use. These usually involving tinkering with our comparisons in some way. I have described several such methods in what follows as well as suggesting how we, as shoppers, should respond.

- Price match guarantees

Many promise to provide a 'price match guarantee' or something similar, hoping to convince us that we needn't bother making price comparisons. After all, if we happen to find the same item at a lower price in another store then the onus is on us to prove this to the first store. This takes time and effort while, even if we're successful, we might only end up paying the same price as we would have done in the second store anyway!

I'm not suggesting that retailers, knowing this, actively take the opportunity to charge relatively high prices. After all, if such a strategy were to be uncovered they could suffer potentially fatal reputational damage. Rather, the 'guarantee' can easily lead us, as customers, to *assume* that it relates to everything the shop sells, whereas in reality several important conditions normally apply. Besides the items being identical, the 'guarantee' may only be valid if the lower priced product comes with the same warranty and/or is not bought online. Even if we know that conditions are likely to be involved, we often can't be bothered to find out exactly what they are.

With so many possible exceptions to price promises it usually makes sense for us to ignore them. This doesn't mean that we should disregard retailers that use this strategy but rather that it would be wise to make comparisons in the normal way when deciding whether to buy from them.

- Automatic renewals

Another well-known tactic we must be wary of is the use of automatic renewals. Here, after a certain period of time, the price we originally paid for something is superseded by another which is almost always higher and often substantially so. We're informed that these schemes, which typically apply to insurance products and items we buy through subscription, will 'make our lives easier'. After all, once we've made our comparisons and selected our preferred item we don't need to repeat the experience unless we choose to do so.

All reputable retailers will let it be known, possibly discreetly, that prices are liable to change when we sign up. But even if we consider this possibility, we're usually able to convince ourselves that our particular choice won't be subject to sizeable price hikes or, more likely, we'll remember to check the new price when the renewal date is close. The problem is we're also inclined to underestimate how busy we are and overestimate how good our memory is when buying these products. True, those selling them will generally inform us of the new price (as well as the existing one in most cases now) close to the renewal date. But, if this is done by email, it's then up to us to make sure it hasn't gone into 'junk', to spot it among our other emails *and* then be bothered to open it.

Money saving experts generally suggest that we never automatically renew, partly because the best deals are often reserved for new customers. At the very least, when buying such an item we need to make a diary note to call the company a couple of weeks ahead of the renewal date to politely express our surprise at the scale of the price rise. When doing so, we can be handsomely rewarded for our efforts.

Although we rarely do it, *automatic saving* can bring greater benefits than automatic buying. If we can afford it, committing ourselves to save a certain amount each month via standing order from our non-interest-bearing current account, allows us to build a nest egg that, more than likely, will provide a pleasant surprise when we eventually need to access it. Our short memories mean that it won't take long to forget that we've done this, while our laziness and busy lives normally make us reluctant to close the account when we do think about it. In this way, we can turn our inherent weaknesses to our advantage.

When setting up such a plan, I suggest that we work out how much we think we can save and then add a bit to it. This is obviously inappropriate if we know that our income is about to fall or our expenditure to rise, but in most cases I suspect that we underestimate how much we're able to save. If it's difficult to begin with, consider whether it would be better to buy fewer frivolous items than save less. Rather than fitting our saving around our spending why not do the opposite?

- 'One-off' price discounts

Hardly a day goes by when we're not bombarded by 'unbeatable' price discounts. The effect is to thrust a price comparison upon us which, as we're now well aware, is fundamental to our buying decision. If we want the item, it's easy to satisfy ourselves that our research is done and make the purchase without concern.

Such price cuts effectively discourage us from comparing the price of two or more competing items by encouraging us to compare two prices for the same item. When we do so, it's tempting to conclude that the product is 'cheap' and we should buy it. But while this *may* be the case it's not necessarily correct and we should still make comparisons with competing products in the normal fashion to check. We mustn't confuse 'cheaper' with 'cheap'.

In the UK at least, this advice is more apt than ever. Before December 2016, the country's Pricing Practices Guide (PPG) advised sellers that to advertise a price cut for a product, they needed to have kept the original price for at least 28 days and that 10% or more of the product range should be discounted. Although not binding in a legal sense, the PPG is generally accepted to represent 'best practice' and widely implemented by retailers. The main change in the new PPG is to move away from such prescriptive rules to a principles based approach where the onus is on the retailer to determine whether they can defend their price strategies if needs be. With greater flexibility, it must be tempting for retailers to test the boundaries.

- Two for the price of one

Retailers frequently complicate our comparisons by offering 'two for the price of one' or a package size that is different to its competitors. This is particularly prevalent in supermarkets and represents a potential trap. We could, for example, be faced with a choice between a packet of pasta weighing 550g at a price of 99p and a different packet weighing 400g priced at 69p. Personally, I need to use a calculator to work out that the latter offers marginally better value for money.

It's excellent news therefore that major UK supermarkets now provide *unit* prices and we should make it a habit to compare items on this basis where possible. Admittedly, we may have to squint to do so given the size of the font typically used, but that's normally easier than making frequent use of a calculator and less financially painful than guessing.

- 'Free shipping' and the power of video

When it comes to making online purchases the following bullet points make for interesting reading.

➢ In 2018, 47% of buyers said that, 'free shipping' was the deciding factor when choosing from whom to buy (US National Retail Association).

➢ People are up to 85% more likely to make a purchase after viewing a product video (Neil Patel Blog).

If we thought about it, we would probably all acknowledge that 'free shipping' usually means that the retailer has included transport costs in the 'headline' price of the product itself. So why does suggesting that it's free have such a big effect on our willingness to buy? It partly illustrates the extraordinary power of zero - we find it incredibly hard to resist something that's purportedly free. It may also reflect a belief that *we* shouldn't be the ones having to pay for shipping, even though if we went to the shop ourselves, bought the item and brought it home we would incur financial costs as well as using valuable time and energy.

The implications are clear. We're not always entirely rational when we shop and need to be more so to improve the quality of some of our decisions. In this instance, we should compare products based on their total price, including shipping, VAT and other extras.

Sometimes the cost of shipping *becomes* zero if we're prepared to spend more than a certain amount. This is good news *if* we genuinely want enough items to take us above the threshold. But don't put an extra thing in the basket, particularly if its price exceeds the shipping cost, just for the sake of achieving free transport. I'm sure many do!

There are probably three reasons why product videos are as influential as they are. First, having opted to invest the time to watch a video, we feel entitled to a return on that investment in the form of ending our search. In other words, we *want* to be persuaded. Second, either consciously or subconsciously, we set aside a certain amount of time for search activity and get itchy feet once that period has expired. Contemplating a video will use up a fair chunk of it. Third, the video serves to bring the product to life, showing us what it can do (often in very controlled circumstances) rather than what it can't, assuming it's produced by the manufacturer or retailer. None of these are particularly good reasons to buy the item.

When watching product videos we need to take account of these biases, while bearing in mind that the persuasiveness of the clips will only increase, particularly as retailers improve their ability to target us as individual buyers. In my opinion, they shouldn't be used as a method to narrow our comparisons by ruling out competitors that don't produce a video or not such a polished version. Where available, watching independent, 'real-life' assessments of the product are obviously to be preferred.

- Playing the percentage game

It's interesting that we're more willing to go the extra mile to save a given amount of money when the product is 'cheap' than when it's 'expensive'. Let's say we've found an item we want to buy, but discover that we could purchase the same thing and save £25 by hopping in a car and driving down the road to another store. Our chances of doing so are far higher if the item is priced at £100 than £1,000. Why? Because we think about the saving we'll make in comparison to the cost of the product we're buying. That is we play the percentage game even though a £25 saving is still a £25 saving whatever it is we're purchasing.

Now think about what happens when we're presented with the opportunity to buy an add-on item to a product. This could be a warranty on a washing machine or leather seats in a new car for example. Again, we're more likely to spend the money if it represents a small proportion of the initial price. What about when we're negotiating the purchase or sale of a house? The odd £5,000 here or there seemingly makes no difference when we're spending or receiving something in the order of, say, £300,000.

In these circumstances, my suggestion is that we don't rush to a decision but briefly consider what we could do with the money we would save. Having done so, if we decide that we're prepared to go to the trouble of traveling to another shop, that the money spent buying an add-on item is better used for something else or it's worth the risk of losing the property we have chosen to bid on, then make the saving. If not, then don't.

- *Selective comparisons*

In his book, "Predictably Irrational,"[1] Dan Ariely illustrated how our buying decisions can be influenced by the specific items included in the comparisons we make. He uses the theoretical case of a US real estate agent choosing to show a potential buyer three houses - one contemporary and two older-style properties. They are equally desirable, except for the fact that one of the older-style properties has a leaking roof. The owner has reduced the price of that property so it's cheaper than the others to reflect this.

Ariely argues that the older-style property with the better roof is the most likely choice. There's nothing to compare the contemporary house with, effectively ruling it out as an option, while the purchaser will conclude that the house with the leaking roof is the worst of the two older-style properties. But what would happen if another contemporary house was added to the mix? Our decision may be completely different.

The author also makes the point that when faced with three variations of the same product we tend to opt for the mid-priced one. Taking the example of a TV purchase, he suggests that the retailer can nudge us towards a particular version by presenting it as the middle one of three. Because we find it impossible to judge between the merits of, say, a 36-inch TV priced at $690, a 42-inch at $850 and a 50-inch at $1,480, we choose the compromise option. Again, the point is that our choice will depend on which TVs happen to be included in the comparison.

We can think about this example in another way. If we didn't have a particular sized TV in mind when entering the store, and the salesperson begins by showing us just the 36-inch and 42-inch versions it would be tough to know which one to select. But if he then introduces the 50-inch option, the decision becomes far easier - we suddenly feel much more inclined to buy the 42-inch.

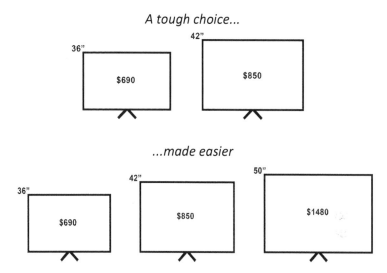

A tough choice...

...made easier

Where a product is physically located in relation to other products can play havoc with the results of our comparisons as well. It's widely recognised that goods placed at eye level sell better than those above or below them for example. Some even suggest that we prefer items that are placed on higher shelves than those towards the bottom - the theory being that we associate 'up' with good and 'down' with bad. Meanwhile, placing a £100 item next to a £500 one will make the former seem cheaper than if a £50 item was nearby - an outcome that is relevant to our buying decisions both at physical stores and online.

We should be mindful of all these effects. Since we generally have to compare a product with something similar for it to even enter our reckoning we will, on occasion, need to widen the range of options from which we choose. Also, having selected what appears to be the compromise option, we may want to test whether our decision remains the same when a different comparison set means it's no longer the mid-priced choice.

At the same time as making this last suggestion, I'm conscious that we could easily spend ages changing our comparison set only to end up more confused than when we started! Often, just ensuring that our comparisons include an even number of options or deciding which characteristics of the product are the most important to us - price, size, weight, appearance etc - before starting the process is sufficient to improve our decision making.

- 'Anchoring'

Whenever we want to buy something we usually have a rough idea of how much we'll need to spend to acquire it. Our expectation is likely to be determined by several different factors, such as our own previous buying experiences, how much a friend paid for the item and how wealthy we are. The price expectation we have then plays an important role in our decisions, effectively 'anchoring' us to a particular number from which we're reluctant to move too far. We compare the actual price we face with that reference point, helping us decide whether we're receiving value for money.

Let's say, for example, that we need a new printer for our computer and, because we haven't bought one for a while, think that it will cost about £50. We then search online and are pleasantly surprised to discover that most printers retail at £25 to £30, with a couple priced at £40 to £50. In these circumstances, we probably won't pay £50 but may well be content to spend £40 - after all, it's quite a bit lower than our initial estimate. But what happens if our price expectation is very different? Perhaps we've spoken to a couple of colleagues who've recently bought 'good' printers for £20. With most of the printers in our search costing £25 to £30, we opt to buy a £25 version, feeling a little hard done by as we have ended up spending £5 more than anticipated.

Put another way, the printer we buy depends partly on the initial price expectation or 'anchor' we have: we'll typically spend more if our anchor happens to be 'high' than if it's 'low'.

Knowing this, we should try to be more open-minded about prices, not letting our prior expectations dictate too much.

It's difficult for retailers to exploit this anchoring effect unless they ask us outright what we expect to pay for an item and we're prepared to provide a truthful answer. The only other thing they can do is use social cues, such as how we dress (assuming we're not shopping online), to make assumptions about our willingness to spend. But beware! Retailers are learning more about the way we shop all the time and using algorithms to predict our spending. It's not inconceivable that online retailers will soon be able to make informed guesses about our price anchors, using them to select what items show up in our searches.

When making major purchases, such as a house or car, we *will* be asked to reveal what we're looking to spend as well as what we expect to get for that money. Again, our (truthful) answers are likely be influenced by our previous experiences, meaning that if, for example, we live in London and are looking to move to Leeds we may be able to get more for our money than we first anticipate. It's in the agent's financial interest, however, to guide us towards properties that offer relatively poor value for money but which still fit our expectations. In these types of situation, we *must* make the effort to research the market thoroughly.

In some cases, we won't have a price expectation at all and can't generate one by looking at the price of similar items. It may be that a manufacturer has launched an entirely new product or we come across an item that's genuinely unique, such as a piece of memorabilia. In these circumstances, the retailer has the power to set our anchor either by assigning a fixed price to the product or, if they're selling by auction, establishing a guide/starting price.

This leaves us vulnerable, particularly as it's been shown that the price we're prepared to pay in such circumstances is highly susceptible to nudges, even entirely random ones. Dan

Ariely illustrated that by simply making people aware of the last 2 digits of their US social security numbers he was able influence how much they bid for a range of different items - those with numbers in the highest 20% offered a remarkable 216-346% above those with the lowest!

Meanwhile, we've all been involved in a price negotiation where the seller sets a 'high' starting price - say £100 - knowing that this will anchor us. We respond by offering half that amount and eventually end up splitting the difference. We walk away thinking we've done well by paying 'just' £75. But what if the initial price was £50 or £200? By changing the anchor, the price we ultimately pay is likely to be very different.

So what should we do in situations where we have little or no idea of what price we should be paying? Be suspicious of the initial/anchor price set by sellers. Unless the item is one of a kind and we don't want to miss out, it's often worth waiting to see how the price develops before taking the plunge. If it's feasible to do so, we could ask how the seller established the starting price, with our actions then guided by the credibility of their answer. We also need to keep an eye out for other, more subtle, forms of price nudges. Finally, in rare instances where we have the opportunity to set the initial price ourselves, be sure to make use of it!

Is help at hand?

I have described several ways in which retailers attempt to influence the results of our comparisons and how we, as shoppers, should react. But there are two additional tools trailered to help us make better decisions - customer reviews and comparison sites. The question is do they properly serve the purpose for which they are intended?

'Customer' Reviews

Reviews have become an increasingly important way of distinguishing between different products that we're comparing, allowing us to learn from other people's (positive and negative) experiences. According to a 2017 survey by Podium, a US tech company, 93% of people said online reviews impacted their purchasing choices, while 82% indicated the content of a review had persuaded them to make a purchase. In the UK, the Competition and Markets Authority has estimated that reviews influence about £23 billion of customer spending every year.

Investigating the trustworthiness of reviews in 2018, the BBC found that, '*fake five-star reviews*' were '*being bought and sold online,*' while uncovering '*online forums where...shoppers are offered full refunds in exchange for product reviews*.' They also suggested that, '*Some US analysts estimate as many as half of the reviews for certain products posted on international websites such as Amazon are potentially unreliable*.' And all this is apparently going on even though the likes of Amazon, Trustpilot and eBay prohibit such activity, pointing out that they use specialist software to screen reviews and remove fakes.

There are several ways to react, the most standard of which is to only read 'verified purchase' reviews as well as putting greater faith in the overall rating given to products that have hundreds of them. We could simply choose not to read the content of top-rated reviews, focusing on 2 to 4 star ones instead. We might also be suspicious of products that have a *relatively* high proportion of 5-star ratings versus 4-star ones, together with quite a few 1 to 3 star ratings: those aiming to boost their score are unlikely to ask for anything other than a 5-star one. Looking at the fictitious customer ratings overleaf, I would be more trustful of the bottom one than the top for this reason.

Customer Reviews

5 Star		70%
4 Star		3%
3 Star		8%
2 Star		9%
1 Star		10%

5 Star		65%
4 Star		18%
3 Star		5%
2 Star		4%
1 Star		8%

When perusing reviews we should also investigate whether there's a common strength or weakness that consumers identify with the product, relating those back to our preferences. It may be, for example, that an item has a relatively high number of 2-star ratings because purchasers are frustrated by having to wait 4-5 days for it to arrive. If we're not in a hurry, then a longer than expected delivery time is obviously irrelevant to us.

In view of the potential trust issues associated with customer reviews, we would be doing a service to our fellow shoppers by providing genuine reviews ourselves...so long as we indicate exactly what it is we like and dislike about the product and award a 4-star rating (out of 5), even if we think it's great!

Comparison websites

Comparison sites cover a growing number of products, including insurance, broadband, travel, utilities as well as some household items. It's estimated that around 11 million UK residents - 20% of the adult population - have used them.

For those unfamiliar with these sites, the best ones will allow consumers to sort competing products from a range of providers in different ways, including by price. By making it far easier for us to compare across the market, they should, in theory, save us time and significantly improve our ability to find the product that best suits our needs and pockets.

Ideal you might think and, in many instances, they can be extremely helpful. There are, however, a few issues to be aware of. In particular, some comparison sites prioritise certain providers above those that may otherwise come out on top in our searches. Also, most won't include every possible provider in the market. The sites make money by taking a small commission from the seller, meaning that those unwilling to pay may be excluded, while those prepared to pay an additional sum could receive preferential treatment. It's also suspected that several sites operate so-called 'Most Favoured Nation' arrangements, whereby providers are prevented from listing lower prices on rival comparison sites.

It's largely for these reasons that the UK's Competition and Markets Authority recommend that we use several platforms before making a final decision. The trouble is, of course, this undermines their purpose somewhat as many of us will not want to spend the time looking through a number of different websites.

More generally, we need to ensure that we're comparing like-for-like. Insurance products are a case in point, given that they frequently have different standard excesses and exclusions. Meanwhile, airline prices usually don't include taxes, which can vary, and hotel rooms may or may not include breakfast. In short, 'headline' prices, often used to rank the alternatives, don't always tell the full story.

In brief

Deciding what to buy and where to buy it will almost always involve making comparisons of one sort or another. Indeed we're usually put off purchasing something if there's nothing to compare it with. Retailers, needing to turn a profit in a highly competitive environment, attempt to influence the results of our comparisons in many, increasingly sophisticated, ways. To make good decisions we should be aware of these.

In particular, product videos and 'free shipping' appear to have bigger effects than they should do; we must set a reminder to check prices ahead of automatic renewals and be prepared to ring the company thereafter; a price reduction means the item is 'cheaper' not necessarily 'cheap' as we often assume; we need to ensure that the particular comparison set we face is not biasing our conclusions too heavily; and, finally, be wary of the effects of our own price anchors as well as those 'kindly' set for us.

Customer reviews and comparison websites are useful additions to the retail landscape, although they too can be subject to unhelpful interference.

Chapter 14

Working

At work, we'll often have to make important decisions: who, among a range of candidates, should we hire? Are we going to change jobs ourselves? Which staff are outperforming and which are underperforming? How can we improve the effectiveness of our annual employee or client conference? Is it sensible to have co-heads managing a team of people? In each case, we'll use comparisons to help make up our minds, but in most instances we can use them more effectively than we do. This chapter explores how.

Another important ingredient in the recipe for employment success is persuasiveness - the ability to convince colleagues, bosses and clients that they should come round to our way of thinking with the minimum of disagreement, threat or upset. There are a wide range of persuasion techniques that involve comparisons and they represent my starting point.

Persuasion by comparison

Whether we're negotiating a multimillion pound contract, implementing unpopular change at work or simply debating something with a colleague, our success will depend partly on our powers of persuasion. In the previous chapter, I outlined various ways in which retailers manipulate our comparisons to persuade us to buy their products and we could employ some of the same tactics ourselves where appropriate. Where they don't apply, there's still plenty we can do.

The door-in-the-face technique

The 'Door-In-The-Face' (DITF) technique involves the persuader initially asking a lot of his 'target', before requesting something less demanding. It's suggested that the target is more likely to agree to the persuaders subsequent request than if he had asked for it to begin with. A host of studies have shown the DITF strategy to be a potent weapon in a persuaders' armoury.

Why does it work? It's commonly suggested that by appearing to compromise the persuader is invoking a powerful social norm - reciprocity - whereby the target feels an obligation to return the favour. After all, 'one good deed deserves another.' We have probably all haggled over the price of something at some point - the seller asks for a particular price which leads us to put in a lower bid. If the seller then reduces the offer price, we usually feel that we should respond to this gesture, upping our bid as a result. The process works in the same way if we're negotiating with a street vendor to buy a T-shirt or we're aiming to get the highest price we can for our office cleaning services.

I believe our compulsion to compare is also influential here. A second, smaller request appears *relatively* undemanding when it's considered in the context of the first one. If we ask somebody to buy ten books and, assuming they reject this appeal, cut that to three, the latter will seem to be a more reasonable number than it otherwise would purely because of the comparison we've imposed (three is a lot less than ten). We'll probably sell more books this way than if we had *started* by asking people to purchase three books. Similarly, if, as the boss, we want somebody to move desks and they are reluctant to do so, we could begin by offering an even worse option than the desk we intend them to use. The latter will represent a comparative improvement on the first offer.

The foot-in-the-door approach

Another well-known persuasion technique, the 'Foot-In-The-Door' (FITD) approach, suggests that we start with a small request, which is highly likely to be accepted, and then increase it. Once we have gained compliance, the argument runs, it's difficult for our target to refuse the second request as this is inconsistent with their first answer. Cognitive dissonance, which we learnt about in chapter 6, would ensue.

At first sight, FITD appears to run counter to my comparison argument - the second request will seem bigger than if it had been asked for initially and is therefore more likely to be refused. But remember the strategy relies on the first, modest, request being *accepted*. If somebody has agreed to buy one book, then they have already indicated that they expect to enjoy it and hence purchasing three is not an unreasonable request. Friends may also be interested in it, for example. If, however, the individual hasn't agreed to purchasing one book, then buying three books is indeed going to seem like quite a big ask!

Social pressure

The influence of social pressure – the desire to 'fit in' - was neatly illustrated back in 2003,[1] when 2,000 randomly selected students at a Swiss university were asked whether they wanted to contribute to Social Funds providing financial support to foreign students and others with financial difficulties. Half of the participants were informed that a relatively high proportion (64%) of the student population contributed and the rest were told that only 46% paid money in. The first number was the figure for the previous semester while the second represented a longer-term average.

According to economic theory, the students would opt not to contribute as it's against their (self) interest to do so. If, however, they were to operate in a purely altruistic manner their contribution rate should decline in tandem with the proportion of people they think are donating: the perceived need to contribute falls as the pool of money rises. So which of the two theories was right? Neither! Instead, those students that were made aware of the 64% contribution rate were *more* likely to contribute than those told that 46% paid. Social pressure, resulting from the comparisons made by the students, proved to be the dominant driver.

The fact that we're more inclined to cooperate when we see others doing so, carries obvious implications for persuasion. If we can demonstrate to our target(s) that they're in good company by accepting our strategy then we'll have a better chance of persuading them. Returning to my example, if we can truthfully say that, '20 people have already bought three books' then we're more likely to be able to sell three books to our target. If we can't, then we could perhaps suggest that, 'several people have indicated that they'll buy more than one book to give as gifts', again assuming this is accurate.

Two-sided arguments

When making the case for or against something, we usually reel off all the points we can think of that support our argument. But given the natural urge to compare, those listening to our case are likely to evaluate the relative merits of the various points we put across, potentially distracting them from the overall argument. They may also become suspicious that we're deliberately excluding important information because it doesn't suit our case, which, of course, is exactly what we're doing on occasion!

To satisfy our audience's desire to compare, therefore, it's a good idea to include some counter-arguments...as long as we go on to answer the issues raised by these points. When arguing in favour of shorter working hours, for example, we might point out that other companies are cutting the length of the working week and it's the socially responsible thing to do, before adding that, 'Some have said the move will harm the profitability of the company by raising costs. In reality, however, productivity is likely to increase as a result of the improvement in staff morale, helping the bottom-line.' We have introduced a comparative argument, but then undermined it.

Limiting the options

In attempting to persuade somebody to choose a particular item, it's important not to give them too many options. By presenting a large range of alternatives, as represented by the left hand section of the image below, rather than a more limited choice (right hand section) researchers have concluded that potential buyers are more likely to walk away with nothing or make poor decisions. This ties in with the argument made in the dating section of chapter 12.

The paradox of choice

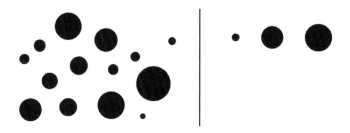

Not only does choice engender confusion sometimes, but we often compare the benefits we have gained from our decision with those we have lost by turning down the other possibilities. We can't help but wonder what we're missing out on. As a result, the more options we offer, the bigger the perceived loss will be, increasing the chance of regret and, in so doing, reducing the chance of repeat business.

The argument - which again runs counter to standard economic theory, suggesting that more choice is always a good thing - has been demonstrated in many different settings from supermarkets selling a variety of different jams to company retirement plans. The latter involved checking the participation of nearly 800,000 US employees in their individual firm's various '401(k)' retirement saving schemes.[2] It found that participation rates were *lower* in those companies that offered their staff a *wider* range of funds from which to select. Where employees were presented with just two options, 75% of them invested on average, while only 60% put money in if they had to choose between nearly 60 funds.

Tipping the balance

A given argument or fact carries far more weight in some circumstances than others. For example, when we have very little knowledge about something, any information whatsoever will have an outsized influence. Similarly, at times when we're struggling to choose between two or more options, which we may know a lot about, just one extra piece of information, however small, can make all the difference. It's analogous to a set of scales which is in perfect equilibrium until a couple of grains of rice is added to one side, tipping the balance.

With this in mind, it's often worth holding back one nugget to use if our target is finding it hard to reach a conclusion. It shouldn't be our strongest argument, which we need to make earlier in the discussion, but something that might otherwise get lost in conversation or quickly forgotten about. This applies both to face-to-face negotiations and those over email.

I refer here to facts, arguments and information but, depending on our specific situation, it could be a (small) price adjustment or a (modest) change to the terms of business that is the more relevant influencer.

'Beauty' contests

Depending on our job, we'll sometimes have to compete with a number of companies to win a contract. Knowing that the decision maker will be comparing our products and services with others, how can we improve our odds of winning the business when making a pitch? Besides those methods I have mentioned, psychological research suggests there are several non-commercial ways to stand out.

➢ We should endeavour to be the first to present or, failing that, the last. Several studies have demonstrated that we're more likely to be remembered that way and, interestingly, for the memory to be attributed to a good performance. This is true even if, in reality, we haven't done that well!

➢ It's useful to find something in common with those we're communicating with, particularly if we differ in obvious and important ways that we can do nothing about. It's essential to establish some sort of connection with our counterparty.

➢ Briefly disclosing personal information about ourselves, such as our interests, will make us appear more human, breaking down barriers and helping us build rapport. Numerous studies have found that this leads to better outcomes.

> Complimenting the strengths or performance of the other party is almost guaranteed to have beneficial effects as long as we're not too sycophantic about it. Even if we're 'just doing our job', we all appreciate being told that we're doing it (or at least aspects of it) well. Yes, many of us find it difficult to give praise, but it's precisely because of this that it's very effective to do so.

> It has also been shown that aesthetics carry more weight than is often assumed. How we present and what materials we use to do so are powerful influencers. The quality of our website and even our business card may have important effects as well.

Decisions, decisions

So far I have considered how we can use comparisons to influence others. They play a different role when it comes to decision making, where we're usually confronted with two or more options, the costs and benefits of which we must compare to come to a conclusion. In doing so, we should be aware of several, potentially costly, traps and some alternative routes we can take to avoid them (as well as ensuring that others are not using any of the persuasion tactics just described, on us!). I begin with the company conference, before moving on to various personnel issues where the main perils lie.

The annual conference - who, what and where?

Big company presentations can serve to inspire staff and clients, presenting the firm in the best possible light. But they can also do the precise opposite and often for easily avoidable reasons.

Have you ever given a presentation or sat listening to one in a room that has far more empty chairs than occupied ones? There's no better way of serving up a damp squib, giving both the speaker and the audience the distinct impression that nobody cares about what's being said. It's a dispiriting feeling for all concerned. However, by simply choosing a smaller room we can help ensure that the same event will be perceived very differently. Even if we're stuck with a larger space than required, we can still affect perceptions by providing fewer chairs and placing them close to each other in front of the podium.

I have attempted to illustrate this point via the images below, with the dashes designed to represent unoccupied chairs and the dots people. Although it doesn't look like it and certainly wouldn't feel like it, the audience is the same size in both pictures. The right hand arrangement will generate a much greater sense of interest and importance.

Controlling the space

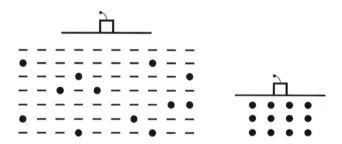

Whatever the situation, it's also a good idea to put out fewer chairs than we think will be required. If the demand for chairs then exceeds the supply of them we can rush to add more, creating the impression that expectations have been surpassed!

At events where there's more than one speaker, it's helpful to give some thought to the order in which they present, assuming logic doesn't dictate the sequence for us. Some people are better presenters than others and comparisons between them are inevitable. If a relatively good speaker *precedes* a relatively poor one, then the poor speaker will be thought of as worse than he would be if the order was reversed. Meanwhile, the comparatively good speaker would be considered even better than he really is if he went second. This is because the first speaker sets the benchmark against which subsequent speakers are then judged. As such, it should suit everybody if the comparatively good speaker follows the relatively poor one...right?

Not necessarily. A problem arises when we consider the *lasting* impression we want to give the audience. As I pointed out earlier, people are more likely to remember what comes first, meaning that, if we're responsible for the whole event, we'll want the better speaker to open not the comparatively poor one.

Fortunately, there are a couple of things we can do to help the relatively poor presenter in these circumstances. Inserting a break in the programme after the first speaker has finished and ensuring that the 'look and feel' of the second speaker's presentational material is even better than that of the first will help both to reduce comparisons and, where they are made, ensure that they are not as stark.

Who deserves what - a role for AI?

If we're 'lucky' enough to have reached a managerial position, we'll need to compare the staff we're responsible for to determine the relative size of their bonuses, who amongst them deserves promotion and, unfortunately on occasion, who to make redundant. For small teams, where we have an intimate knowledge of what everybody is doing and how they're performing, such personnel decisions are usually reasonably straightforward (although not necessarily uncontentious). But where we're accountable for large teams, particularly geographically diverse ones, it can be much trickier.

Indeed so much so the issue is helping incentivise the development of new, technologically advanced, methods to monitor employees' activities far more easily and scientifically than was previously possible. The question is will they resolve the problem to everyone's satisfaction?

Existing GPS technology already permits companies to track the routes and location of vehicles, while some firms use Radio Frequency Identification (RFID) badges to keep tabs on the exact whereabouts and movements of their staff at work. However, the introduction of Artificial Intelligence systems - defined by the Royal Society of Arts, Manufactures and Commerce (RSA) as '*Tasks performed by computer software* (bundles of algorithms) *that would otherwise require human intelligence*' - could be about to take things to a new level.

A 2017 RSA report presented a couple of examples of novel AI 'surveillance' tools fresh to the market.[3] So-called "Sociometric Badges," allow employers to analyse various characteristics of their employees' voices to investigate the quality of workplace interactions. The technology can learn from its own experiences. Another new piece of software logs exactly what staff are doing on their office computers, with an AI system then crunching the data to create a measure of productivity for each individual. It flags up those that are underperforming, allowing managers to take the appropriate action.

The retail sector has been an early adopter of AI, making it a useful test case for those following on. Many large stores now use algorithms to collect and monitor data regarding aspects of an employee's work, including their performance on checkout tills and the speed with which they pick items for home delivery. It's claimed that such systems help create organisational efficiencies and improve decision making to the benefit of managers, customers and the bottom-line. Good news, assuming this is right. But what about the impact on the staff themselves?

A recent study investigated the effects in a sizeable store located in the Republic of Ireland.[4] Several problems became apparent. In particular, the systems led employees to feel that their primary purpose at work was to *'generate data',* rather than to help customers directly. This sense was reinforced by the fact that some activities, including building customer relations, weren't covered in their appraisals because they *'couldn't be coded.'* The result was that staff felt dissatisfied - *'small cogs in a large wheel'* - lacking motivation and divorced from the reasons for their efforts.

If this is typical of the impact of AI, then managers will be left with a choice: prioritise efficiency gains, including the ability to compare the performance of individual employees, over staff morale or vice versa. In roles where little or no interaction with customers and other staff is required to do the job, I imagine that 'Big Brother' will generally win the day, while, if the opposite is the case, it won't or at least shouldn't.

AI (and robots) are evidently still a long way from being able to satisfactorily measure, let alone replace, many human skills. Assuming this remains the case and automation continues to destroy mundane tasks in favour of those requiring caring, creative and other truly human qualities, then an interesting conclusion follows - *fewer* employees may be subject to 'Big Brother' surveillance techniques than many currently believe likely.

While this is good news in some respects it suggests that employers' difficulties in objectively comparing the performance of staff will remain unresolved. It also means that age-old problems of real or perceived inequity among workers will continue. It's not just as children that we use comparisons to check whether we're being badly treated: in the first part of the book, I pointed to a study that showed how a worker's productivity dived when he felt he was unfairly treated relative to a colleague.

As *managers,* we must anticipate such comparisons and respond accordingly. Apart from requesting employees keep details of their pay and conditions secret, we should always justify our decisions. We may also want to weigh up the potential benefits of encouraging competition between employees against the costs this may have for working relationships within the firm. A 2012 US research paper, exploring the effects of social comparisons on trust between workers, concluded that where they compete with each other for promotions and pay rises they were more wary of confiding in each other and less confident in their colleagues' abilities to represent their interests.[5]

Another idea, designed to muddy the comparison waters but with other benefits as well, is to offer employees a *choice of* rewards at bonus time. We could ask them to select between additional cash, shares, extra holiday or a combination of all three. I'm aware companies like to retain control, but why not give workers a little more autonomy in this respect? Finally, we need to carefully 'manage' the expectations of our staff, keeping in mind that everyone compares actual outcomes with their anticipation of reality. As I alluded to earlier, undershooting expectations is never a good thing.

As *employees*, we must be careful what we wish for. By appealing for impartial measurement tools we may, if successful, become extremely unpopular with our colleagues judging by the Irish retail example I referred to! Where our bosses continue to operate imprecise assessment methods, we sometimes just have to play the game, passing on any positive feedback we receive to them, for example.

Are two heads better than one?

At times when two people are clamouring to be top-dog, companies will often attempt to appease both parties by making them co-heads. But this often causes more problems than it solves, partly because those making the decision again fail to take proper account of the power of comparisons.

In theory, the all but inevitable competition that emerges between co-heads could serve to push them both to deliver better results to the benefit of the company. In practice, as we've just seen, competition often creates damaging trust issues as well as constant comparisons designed to ascertain who's outperforming who. They'll often waste time and effort attempting to convince *their* boss(es) that *they* are the one doing the better job, possibly working to undermine each other in the process. Even when each co-head has been given specific parts of the business to manage, turf-wars are common. In one firm where I worked, the co-heads wouldn't even agree to meet in the other's office, presumably for fear of being perceived to be the less dominant of the two! Suffice to say it didn't make for particularly effective team leadership.

There are, of course, occasions when co-heads do work well together, but the very fact that the literature focusses almost exclusively on how to make a success of it, suggests that this is more the exception than the rule. A 2010 study[6] by Maria Arnone and Stephen Stumpf, who interviewed many co-heads as part of their research, summed up the issue perfectly...

'While the structure can be a lasting one, adopting co-head roles is best thought of as an interim strategy that requires careful consideration of corporate context and competitive environment and the risk factors involving the personal dynamics of shared leadership.'

In my opinion, the single biggest risk factor is the misuse of comparisons in these situations, something the literature fails to give much, if any, explicit attention to. If we're deciding whether to create a co-head arrangement or being considered as a co-head ourselves we needn't make the same mistake. We should think carefully about how we can discourage unhelpful comparisons as well as deal with their effects before implementing or agreeing to the structure. Alternatively, if we're being managed by co-heads then illustrating the benefits of teamwork by collaborating effectively with our immediate colleagues is something positive we can contribute.

Who to hire?

In deciding who to recruit, we generally do one of two things. Either compare each candidate with the other candidates competing for the job or make a comparison between the aspirant and the particular individual they will be replacing.

The first method can create problems if we select from an inappropriate pool of people. By doing so, the candidate we decide is the best of the bunch may still be completely unsuitable for the job. We could, for example, opt to restrict our search to applicants from top UK universities when we don't require somebody at that level of academic competence. Another mistake is to narrow the field to those who have similar experience and background to ourselves, when we really need somebody who has a completely different grounding and a complementary skill set.

When an employee is leaving, what we look for in the replacement will often depend on whether the departing individual is deemed to have been a success or failure. In the case of the former, we'll tend to search for somebody who is all but identical, only to be disappointed when we fail to find that person. We usually end up with the 'second best' solution - clearly not an ideal way to begin a working relationship. In the case of the latter, we're drawn to individuals that have the polar opposite characteristics of the individual we're replacing, forgetting to test whether our choice is also strong in aspects of the job that the outgoing employee did well.

It seems to me that when *any* job vacancy arises we should explicitly determine the most important attributes necessary to fulfill the role and then rigorously test for those skills in the candidates (see table below for an example). If it's excellent technical knowledge and good communication skills that we're after, this will require the use of very different evaluation methods than those designed to detect strong leadership abilities and a willingness to work long hours. If we can't find anybody that fits the criteria well, we should seriously consider whether we're looking in the right place, shifting the search accordingly.

Main Attributes for the Job	How to Test
Excellent presentation skills	Ask candidates to prepare and give a 10-minute presentation on a subject of relevance to the job
Get on well with different types of people	Request a variety of colleagues to interview candidates. Ask for examples when the candidate has dealt well with 'difficult' people. Present different scenarios and ask how they would make a success of them
Prepared to work long hours	Make it clear this is what the job involves and ask candidates for their thoughts
A willingness to do the same or similar job for 2-3 years	Try to ascertain how ambitious the candidates are and how long they've stayed with their previous employers

Many companies, particularly those that receive a large quantity of applicants, use IQ-type tests as a means of narrowing the field before moving to interviews or other forms of scrutiny. While I appreciate that some form of initial screening is required in these circumstances, we need to be aware that filtering by IQ can bring unintended consequences. By examining a very specific form of intelligence, which may or may not be that pertinent to the role, the firm is in danger of excluding those who perform relatively poorly on such tests but excel in other areas more crucial to the job. Traditional intelligence tests obviously can't measure softer skills such as empathy, adaptability, dedication and communication.

This doesn't necessarily mean abandoning IQ tests altogether. Rather, they shouldn't be the *only* means by which we include some individuals and exclude others. As recruiters, we owe it to the wider company as well as prospective employees to devise and implement methods that investigate the strength of a range of relevant skills in applicants. Academics, tech companies and HR departments actively involved in such work are to be encouraged in their efforts.

Time for a change?

Rather than comparing the suitability of candidates for a job, there may be times when we compare our own job with a different one. This could be because we're bored where we are, we're not getting on with our boss or, if we're lucky, another company is offering us more money and longer holidays. Several push and pull factors might be at play.

When deciding whether to stay put or depart to pastures new it's very easy to believe that 'the grass is greener on the other side.' This well-known idiom, which can apply to our thought processes in all sorts of different situations, suggests that we're often too keen to exchange what we *know* is bad for something that we *assume* will be better. We compare the pros and cons of our existing job with those of a potential new one, donning rose-tinted glasses when considering the latter. Put another way, our comparisons are biased in a way that makes a job move seem more attractive than perhaps it is in reality.

In chapter 12, I described our tendency to make fundamental attribution errors when driving - to reach for the simple answer (blaming mistakes on the 'stupidity' of another driver) when we don't have the full facts. The risk is that we do something similar when opting to change jobs, attributing our discontent to the job, boss or company when the real problem lies with ourselves. It wouldn't be so bad if we then realised this was the case and worked to resolve the underlying issue. Sadly, however, we have a nasty habit of repeating the mistake, frequently swapping jobs in a fruitless hunt for a 'happy' working life.

This, of course, is not to suggest that we should remain in the same job come what may. Part of what makes us human is our innate sense of restlessness. It's what pushes us to progress as an individual and, collectively, as a society and we need to embrace it sometimes.

So what's it to be - should we stick or twist? To help us decide it's vital to determine what's most important to us in a job, comparing our current position with the alternative based on these priorities having removed our rose-tinted glasses. When doing so, we'll inevitably be faced with various uncertainties about the new role, not all of which can be resolved by asking the right questions of our potential new employer. The thing is there's also likely to be a lot more uncertainty surrounding our current job than we typically assume. A host of things can and frequently do happen to change our current situation and outlook. We could come into work tomorrow to find that our boss has resigned, the company is being taken over or we're being considered for a new position in the same firm for example. To assume that the future will remain the same as the past is almost always a mistake.

In circumstances where we're paralysed by uncertainty, we'll need to make a judgement call. All I would note, is that we're more likely to make a success of whatever decision we reach when our expectations are appropriate and we commit to our choice.

In brief

The use of appropriate comparisons can improve our powers of persuasion at work (and elsewhere). Making requests seem smaller than they are, exerting social pressure, using two sided arguments and/or limiting choice are among the many comparison related techniques that help us subtly influence others. At the same time, understanding how we can stand out from the crowd when others are using comparisons to make judgements could make the difference between winning and losing a contract or success and failure when attempting to land a job.

We sometimes use comparisons in a way that *reduce* the chance of making the right decisions at work. This is particularly true when it comes to deciding who to hire and whether to change jobs ourselves. It's also easy to underestimate the power of comparisons when organising the annual company conference, establishing a co-head arrangement or determining bonuses and promotions. Artificial Intelligence systems have a long way to go before they're capable of providing a satisfactory solution to the last of these issues. There are, however, other methods we can use.

Chapter 15

Sporting

Much of what it takes to be successful in competitive games and sport relates to our physical attributes and technical abilities. But psychological techniques are now widely recognised as having an important role to play as well, explaining the growth of the sports psychology industry. Whether we're participating in a World Cup Final or a Saturday afternoon league, having the right mental approach can make the difference between winning and losing. This is where comparisons come in. Competition inevitably involves comparisons and comparisons inevitably influence our mindset. Not surprisingly, therefore, training our brain to make better comparisons in a sporting context can give us an edge.

Comparisons are not just relevant to those directly involved in playing sport but also to those of us watching from the sidelines. As a coach or somebody attempting to forecast sporting outcomes, for gambling or other purposes, we use comparisons to judge players, teams and managers. Errors, often with expensive consequences, are very common in these circumstances but can be reduced by applying more appropriate comparisons. We'll see how later on.

Comparisons and sporting performance

There are several ways in which the comparisons we make affect the sporting performances we produce.

Self-assessment

The whole idea of competitive sport is to test ourselves against opponents, effectively comparing our abilities with others to see who comes out on top. We draw conclusions about ourselves when doing this, which, irrespective of whether they are correct, will have meaningful implications for our subsequent performance. The following are a couple of examples, illustrating the point.

Having lost to a team below us in the League we conclude that, 'We must be rubbish.' Feeling despondent and suffering a lack of confidence we lose the next game, seemingly supporting our negative view. Alternatively, after thrashing an opponent we decide that, 'We're fantastic' and don't bother to prepare properly for the next match. We're overconfident and are defeated badly. To summarise...

<u>**Current Situation**</u>

We compete and compare...

...often drawing unhelpful conclusions

We internalise those conclusions...

...*reducing* the chances of winning next time

Sporting comparisons, like others, can either be destructive or constructive. Both of my examples obviously fall in to the first category, serving to harm our chances of future success. But this needn't be the case.

An important lesson of the first part of the book is that when comparing ourselves with others we should do so for analytic purposes rather than to reach quick and easy summary judgements about our skills or lack of them. In a sporting context, one option, adopted by many, is to ask 'Why did we get the result we did?' or words to that effect. The trouble is this is unlikely to get us very far, often creating more questions than answers.

Taking my first example where we've lost to a more lowly placed team (or individual), there could be a host of possible explanations for the outcome. Our opposition's League position may have been deceptive and we read too much into it. Perhaps they had previously experienced a spate of injuries to key players or were underprepared in previous matches. Alternatively, for whatever reason, they may just happened to have played well against us and will revert to type next time. As for our own performance, we might conclude that, 'The conditions didn't favour us,' 'We were just unlucky' or 'Too many of our players had an off-day.'

There are other problems with this approach as well. In close matches where 'fine margins' determine the result, we can end up attributing the result to one small error, forgetting about other blunders (or moments of brilliance) from both teams that could easily have made the difference on another day. Even the world's best players make mistakes and it's impossible for any individual or team to eliminate them altogether - trying to do so will prove endlessly frustrating. Michael Jordan, probably the best basketball player of all time, famously pointed out that he had missed more than 9,000 shots and lost almost 300 games during his career.

We also make hugely simplifying assumptions about what, in practice, are usually highly complex, dynamic and interactive situations. 'If we had made that tactical change sooner we wouldn't have lost' or 'If our striker had been fit we would have won.' In reality, there's no way of knowing how the game would have panned out if the alteration had come earlier or the player was available.

To be clear, it's rarely straightforward to *accurately* determine the reasons for success or failure in sport, which is largely why we jump to the easy, albeit frequently unhelpful, conclusions we do.

Whether we win, lose or draw, a much better approach is to ask ourselves questions such as 'What did we do badly? What worked? What can we improve on? What can we learn from the opposition?' These stop us from concentrating on things we can't influence, allowing us to focus on controllable elements of our performance. As such, we're far more likely to elicit answers that will help us improve. 'We didn't close down their star player quickly enough and will need to do that better next time' or 'We were really good in open play but our set plays weren't great. We should practise those more.'

A Better Approach

We compete and compare...

...asking ourselves 'what did we do badly' and 'what did we do well?'

We act on the conclusions...

...*increasing* the chances of winning

The same questions are not just useful to address once the match has finished but during intervals in the game as well, irrespective of the current score. Although there's only a certain amount we can adjust at these times, we may still be able to change the course of the match. 'We committed too many people forward on a couple of occasions. We need to be careful not to leave ourselves open to counterattacks in the second half.'

During matches (and *before* they begin if we are knowledgeable about the opposition), we can also use comparisons to ascertain the relative strengths and weaknesses of the person or team we're facing: the aim being to adapt our game plan accordingly. For instance, 'Their striker will tear our defence apart. We need somebody marking him the whole time and will have to double-up when he's getting close to goal.' 'The opposition's left-back is worse than their right-back. We should concentrate our attacks down that side of the pitch.'

If our comparisons create either a sense of intimidation or overconfidence then we know that we're using them inappropriately.

Chasing v leading

Sportspeople often argue that staying at the 'top' is far more difficult than getting there, while chasing is often easier than leading: after all, when we're behind our objective is crystal clear - improve. These sentiments are heard throughout the sporting world, although, judging by the *consistent* success of some, they can be overcome. Again, appropriate comparisons are key.

I have argued that the rightful purposes of our upward comparisons is to learn from and be motivated by them. But what if we're in a winning position or deem ourselves to be the best? We may decide that there are no upward comparisons we *can* make, often creating complacency and a feeling that there is nothing more to achieve. Meanwhile, our downward comparisons may generate a sense of supremacy, which, whether consciously or subconsciously, can also lead to laziness - 'I'm so much better than the competition I can afford to take it easy for a bit.'

Mia Hamm, the now retired US soccer legend, was well aware of the dangers of such thoughts and how to deal with them. The following are quotes from her...

- *'Celebrate what you've accomplished but raise the bar a little higher each time you succeed.'*

- *'Take your victories, whatever they may be, cherish them, use them, but don't settle for them.'*

- *'You don't just want to beat a team. You want to leave a lasting impression in their minds so they never want to see your face again.'*

- *'Many people say I'm the best women's soccer player in the world. I don't think so. And because of that, someday I just might be.'*

I suspect Tiger Woods would agree with these sentiments bearing in mind his extraordinary record of having won 14 of his 15 golfing majors (at the time of writing) when leading going into the final round. He also holds the record for the most consecutive weeks as the world's No.1 ranked player – 281, amounting to nearly five and a half years.

The lesson seems to be to update our target(s) once we have met the original goal or are close to achieving it. If we're leading at half-time we could aim to win the second half as well or if we have topped the league and can't be promoted to a higher one our new objective is to win it by a bigger margin next time.

Also, whether we're expected to win, are winning or have already won it *is* still possible to compare upwards. There *will* be better individuals or teams that we can learn from and be inspired by. Even those who are not as good as us overall, can still be better at particular aspects of the game.

The importance of 'Psychological Flexibility'

The nature of sporting competition is that circumstances change rapidly and often in unexpected directions. We can find ourselves winning one minute but losing the next, a player may get injured or an important decision could go against us. In each case, it's hugely advantageous to be able to adjust our mindset quickly and effectively. So-called 'Psychological Flexibility' is a highly effective tool, particularly when the momentum in a game shifts.

There are number of ways to deliver the required mindset change. Thinking and expressing some of the thoughts I described earlier can be helpful, while many favour a 'mindfulness' approach as embodied by Acceptance and Commitment Therapy (ACT) for example. Rather than actively trying to alter our thinking this involves 'observing' our unhelpful thoughts, letting them wash over us and then committing to constructive behaviours.

Overleaf, I have provided generic examples of the sort of constructive thoughts and actions we could adopt when a game situation *changes*. It's important to note how similar they are whether we're winning or losing.

Game Change	Unhelpful Feelings	Constructive Questions	Constructive Thoughts & Actions
From losing to *winning*	Superiority & complacency	What can we do to protect and stretch our lead?	1. Stop thinking about the final result 2. Exploit a pause to refocus 3. Continue with what's working well 4. Anticipate the opposition's response & make changes if appropriate 5. Concentrate on the basics
From winning to *losing*	Inferiority & doom	What can we do to get back in the game?	1. Stop thinking about the final result 2. Exploit a pause to refocus 3. Continue with what's working well 4. Make a tactical and/or personnel change if appropriate 5. Trust team mates & training 6. Adopt positive body language

Training comparisons & pressure situations

Before we can hope to compete successfully we must train well. Even the most naturally gifted sportspeople can't expect to triumph without honing their skills and improving their fitness. But training is also of psychological benefit, providing confidence that we're fit and ready to perform to the best of our abilities. In determining how much training to undertake many top sports men and women compare their regime to that of their competitors with the explicit aim of doing more than them. Whether their assessment is accurate or not, they need to *believe* that they are out-training their opposition. Speaking to the BBC, Sir Bradley Wiggins, the 2012 Tour de France winner, recounted an experience he had when he was 17...

'I rode from London to Rye on the south coast on Christmas day...I remember thinking the World Junior Championships were the following August and none of my competitors would be doing this on Christmas day. I loved the idea of it. That's my motivation.'

I'm not suggesting that we need go to quite these extremes(!), but if self-doubt and motivation are lacking, comparisons of this sort can provide a powerful remedy. They are not the only useful training comparisons we can make either. Comparing what we're currently able to do with what we used to be able to achieve serves as a useful reminder that we're moving in the right direction. Meanwhile, setting challenging training targets for our future-selves to accomplish can provide us with the drive to meet new, more exacting standards.

A further comparison related training technique that brings psychological, as well as physical and technical benefits is to make aspects of our practise *more* challenging than the real thing. Athletes competing in 3,000 metre races will often run much longer distances in training; some golfers practise with heavier clubs; cricketers like to use smaller bats and marksmen aim at tinier targets. If we can still do well under these circumstances then the events themselves should seem easier. By contrast, if confidence is a problem it might be helpful to do the opposite for a while: make our training *easier* than the real thing by using larger goals or practising against weaker opposition for example.

Although these methods will help, one thing training can't do is fully replicate the pressures involved in real-life, match situations. While stress brings out the best in some it can badly undermine the performance of others. What we deem to be an easy skill to complete during practise can suddenly become extremely difficult when there's more riding on the outcome. It's what lies behind the 'yips' in golf or 'dartitis' in darts, often preventing good sportspeople from becoming excellent ones.

The lack of pressure in training compared with actual competition has led many to argue that certain skills, such as penalty taking, are not worth practicing at all - we're simply wasting our time so doing. I disagree. Training not only improves motor skills and muscle memory but, as we have seen, reduces self-doubt. In fact, the greater the pressure the more important it is to feel that taking a penalty, or performing technical aspects of any sport for that matter, is second nature. Not having to worry about where we're going to aim or how long our run-up should be takes some of the pressure out of the situation. Oddly, the same people recommending that we shouldn't practise penalties fail to argue that it's futile rehearsing 30 metre passes, although the logic of their argument surely suggests that they should.

Nevertheless, if pressure is a major problem we will need to implement other stress-busting, confidence-building techniques such as those I described in chapter 8.

Comparisons & sporting judgement

So much for the role comparisons can play in improving our sporting performance. What about their influence when it comes to our sporting judgement?

An important part of coaching and team selection is judging the merits and deficiencies of various players. Such assessments also form the basis of many gambling decisions, which can extend beyond a verdict on individual players to teams and managers as well. Coming to a judgement usually involves comparisons, which, as usual, can easily mislead. There are several common mistakes to be wary of and although I can't guarantee we'll always make the right decision having learnt the lessons, we should at least be able to avoid some comparison related clangers.

The World Cup effect

Have you ever been blown away by the ability of an individual footballer or team during a World Cup match only to be disappointed by their performance on another occasion? If the answer is 'yes' then you are by no means alone. Indeed even highly experienced managers frequently make the same mistake, buying World Cup 'stars' who suddenly become 'very average' when they play in a regular domestic league. The same effect can also lead us to place a misguided bet on a player or team. We assume that if they have performed brilliantly against one team they are bound to do just as well against another. Unfortunately, it doesn't always work quite like that.

One of the unusual things about World Cups is that they can pitch a good team against a fairly poor one, making players within the good team appear to be much better than is normally the case. Why is this? Because our judgement is relative: the players look great *compared* with the opposition when the opposition is significantly worse. As soon as the same players come up against other players of similar or higher standard, which will generally be the case in domestic Leagues, then we usually wonder what all the fuss was about. Similarly, if we were to play a match against a team of 8 year olds we might give the impression of being a capable sports person but that doesn't mean that we actually are!

I've labelled this the World Cup effect but it applies to any competition where a player/team comes up against another player/team who is at a very different level. A much better assessment is gained when they are competing against others at the equivalent level of competition.

The curse of legends

When it comes to judging managers and coaches, we typically compare the team's performance under their watch with what's gone before. Most of the time this doesn't create any particular issues but there are occasions when it does.

Since Sir Alex Ferguson retired as manager of Manchester United in 2013, the football club is now on to its fifth replacement (one of which was a 'caretaker'). The main problem for his successors is that they find themselves competing against a legend. In his 27 years as 'The Gaffer', Sir Alex won 38 trophies including 13 Premier League Titles, five FA Cups and two UEFA Champions Leagues: an astonishing legacy which has created hugely elevated expectations and, as a result, a poisoned chalice for those who have followed the great man.

Memories of the 27 years that preceded Ferguson's reign either don't exist or may have faded in the case of older supporters. A quick summary may be of interest, therefore. During the period, Manchester United's average finishing position in the top division of English football was between seventh and eighth. The team won the title just twice and were even relegated on one occasion. They scooped one European Cup (the equivalent of today's Champions League).

The combination of this history, Sir Alex's once in a generation abilities and the big improvements made by other clubs suggests that Manchester United is far from certain to finish in the top four every season. And yet, failing to do so, almost guarantees a P45 for the latest incumbent of the managerial hot seat.

If you think that's bad take a look at what's happened at Nottingham Forest, where the ghost of another managerial marvel, Brian Clough, continues to spook his replacements. In an incredible 18 years at the club, Clough took the team from the second tier of English football, which it was not unused to, to the first, winning four League Titles and back-to-back European Cups. Since Clough left in 1993, Forest have run through 31 managers (including caretakers) and won nothing of major significance. It hasn't even featured in the top division since 1999.

The lesson? Success is great but it often generates unfair comparisons and hence unrealistic expectations that can last for years if not decades. Although it's impossible to know whether the departure of a great manager means the team's subsequent performances are worse than if he hadn't been there in the first place, it *is* clear that the pressure on those that follow is ramped up enormously.

Similar effects are witnessed when it comes to individual players as well. If somebody is perceived to be replacing a 'star' then comparisons and additional pressure will follow. It may be the best part of 50 years since Pelé stopped playing for the Brazilian national team, but anybody wearing his iconic Number 10 shirt is still compared with the footballing genius. This is an extreme example but comparisons of a similar nature can occur at any level in any sport. Whether the person sinks or swims will depend partly on their ability to handle the situation.

Absence CAN make the heart grow fonder

Isn't it weird how the substitutes or injured players of a team suddenly become a lot better when their colleagues are performing poorly? We convince ourselves that if they were playing rather than sitting on the sidelines the game situation would be very different.

This is another comparison effect. In the circumstances I've described, we *know* that the players on the pitch are performing poorly, meaning that those that are not actively participating improve, albeit only by comparison. They obviously don't get better in an absolute sense, but, as we've seen in other circumstances, we often confuse relative with absolute. The result is that if the replacements do enter the fray they frequently disappoint. We forget that there's usually a performance related reason why they are sitting on the bench in the first place.

This works the other way round as well - substitutes seem to become worse when their team is playing well. It's noticeable how reluctant coaches are to 'change a winning team' even when elements of it will, from an unbiased perspective, probably be improved by a replacement. It's often not until the particular weakness is exposed by the opposition that an adjustment is made, by which time it may be too late.

Nationalistic dangers

Our assessment of players and teams can be influenced by whether we support them or not. We tend to inflate the ability of those we favour compared to the opposition, biasing what should be an impartial judgement if we're placing a bet. This effect is most obvious when it comes to national competitions, with England's run to the 2018 men's football World Cup semi-final a case in point.

In the group stage, England beat Tunisia and Panama but lost to Belgium. This was enough to see the team through to the last 16, where they defeated Columbia (on penalties, having practised them!), before beating Sweden in the quarters. By the time of the semi-final against Croatia, the vast majority of my compatriots were convinced that, *'Football was coming home!'* There were, however, several reasons not to be quite so optimistic. The team's performances had, to that point, left plenty to be desired; Croatia was looking like a much better team; England had only played one top ten ranked team in progressing to the semis (Belgium); and France and Belgium (the other semi-finalists) were both evidently superior teams.

Even Mark Lawrenson, former Liverpool player turned respected BBC pundit, who represented the Republic of Ireland at international level, had been caught up in the tide of enthusiasm. Speaking ahead of the Croatia match he said...

'I just have a feeling that England will find a way to win. Sometimes I think these things are written - and the way this tournament has opened up for England is one of the reasons it feels like this is their time...While England's results have been a lot better than their performances, that is not a bad thing in a tournament like this.'

Any attempt to provide rational analysis had clearly long since gone! More interestingly, the betting odds - which partly reflect the relative weight of money placed on the possible outcomes - saw England priced at 11/8 to triumph in normal time (a bet of £8 giving a profit of £11 if successful) and Croatia at 13/5. This equates to a 42% probability of England winning in 90 minutes compared to just 28% for Croatia. It was also notable that English players dominated the list of those thought most likely to score the first goal. 'Nobody to score' in normal time had shorter odds than Croatia's most prolific striker!

As it turned out England *were* first to score (although the goal came from an unfancied player), but 'we' still lost the match 2-1. This is not to suggest that an England loss was inevitable but rather that the odds almost certainly reflected a lot of 'nationalistic betting'. Of course, many Croatians may also have been betting on their team for nationalistic reasons, but, given the relative sizes of the two populations, I suspect that those doing so were heavily outnumbered.

Confirmation bias

Confirmation bias often plays a role in this nationalistic effect. It suggests that once we have concluded that a team or player is good we'll favour evidence that supports it, while dismissing that which doesn't. In essence, we compare any new information we receive with our belief and only store it if it fits with our existing view. This again brings dangers if we're making what should be unbiased judgement calls.

Let's assume we watch a rugby match where a player we like is largely anonymous in the first half but does better in the second. The chances are we'll give much greater credence to his second half performance and leave the match more convinced than ever that our view is correct. Alternatively, we may be a spectator at Wimbledon where our favourite tennis player combines a lot of unforced errors with several great ground strokes. Win or lose, our memory is of the things she's done well.

In both situations, if we had the opposite view of the player to begin with we would have reached the opposite conclusion about their performance. This phenomenon helps explain why two people watching the same match can reach completely different verdicts about the performance of the individual players or teams involved. Better decision making requires us to at least consider alternative arguments.

A variation on the theme can occur when we gamble on something unusual happening. It may be, for example, that we're convinced a team will come back from a losing position to win against the odds. The chances are that our gut feeling stems from memories of (rare) occasions when this has happened, while we have forgotten about the (far more frequent) times when it hasn't. By all means, place the bet, but do so based on more solid reasoning than selective memories.

In brief

Comparisons are a vital part of competitive sport, influencing both our chances of winning and how we judge players and teams.

Too often, the results of our sporting comparisons lead us to feel intimated or overconfident in similar fashion to the processes described in the first part of the book. We also spend too much time discussing what might have been, instead of focussing on controllable elements of our performance and how we can adapt our play to exploit the opposition's comparative weaknesses.

The dynamic nature of sporting competition means that an ability to rapidly adjust our mindset is another useful psychological tool. It will help us counter complacency and respond effectively when falling behind. Comparing our training regime with those of our competitors and ensuring that training is harder than the real thing can make a positive difference as well.

As in so many aspects of life, our sporting judgements are riddled with biases resulting from poor comparisons. For the sake of coherent sporting conversation, effective team management and, perhaps most importantly, our wallets it's helpful to be aware of the various hazards.

Chapter 16

Investing

When it comes to investing our hard-earned money, comparisons are again commonplace and yet frequently unhelpful, often luring us into what turn out to be financially painful decisions. Watching others 'get rich' as we languish 'out of the market' might see us rush in just at the wrong time; we assess the quality of our investments on the basis of whether they've gone up or down, failing to 'benchmark' appropriately; we compare the past performance of financial instruments as a means to determine which to buy and are disappointed when our picks perform poorly; we postpone investment decisions, in the optimistic belief that the future will be less uncertain than the present; and we respond differently to losses and gains when it's unwise to do so. A deeper understanding of the effects of our comparisons and how we can improve them will ensure we make better choices.

Fearful investing

In the first part of the book, I referred to the 'Fear of Missing Out' (FOMO) as a factor behind social media addiction but it's also highly pertinent when it comes to investing. We dislike watching others become richer, particularly when, we surmise, it's so easy to replicate their success simply by buying what they're buying. We dread being the only one of our peer group to have missed out on an 'obvious' get rich quick scheme, perhaps imagining them zooming around in their luxury new cars as we're left trailing in their exhaust fumes still driving our battered old bangers! In some cases, the pressure to participate will be ramped up further by people explicitly urging us to 'get in while you can' or it's 'a no-brainer' to buy now.

Our FOMO is this context is really a Fear of *Not* Making Money (FONMM) and it can all but force us to follow suit, often against our better judgement. Even the most experienced are sucked in occasionally. When the share prices of tech companies exploded in the late-1990s dot-com bubble I remember listening to normally conservative analysts excitedly recommending the purchase of what could only be termed extraordinarily expensive stocks on the basis that they were marginally less expensive than some others! 'Yes, it's pricey but it can still get a lot more expensive' was a familiar refrain at the time which many 'long-term' professional investors literally bought, partly for fear of underperforming competitors. Those that held out were frequently lambasted for doing so.

FONMM is most intense and widespread during asset price bubbles - defined by Investopedia as '*A surge in the price of assets, such as shares, property and precious metals, unwarranted by the fundamentals and driven by exuberant market behaviour.*' As we buy with our eyes closed and fingers firmly crossed, determined not to miss out on 'the next big thing' FONMM can itself serve to inflate the bubble further. The main problem with bubbles is that they inevitably burst at some unpredictable point leaving the vast majority of us either nursing losses or smaller gains that we had imagined. Envy quickly turns to regret...until, that is, the next 'unmissable' investment opportunity arrives and we're informed 'it's different this time.'

We usually react in the opposite manner when asset prices are *falling* sharply. Here our Fear Of Losing Money (FOLM) takes over. We sell or don't dare to buy, preferring to wait for greater clarity, while metaphorically shaking our heads at those 'foolish' enough to have bought 'too soon'. This tendency is again so powerful and extensive that it can prove self-fulfilling...for a while. In these circumstances, regret materialises when we dismiss the turning point as a 'dead cat bounce', missing what frequently turns out to be the sharpest price gains of the cycle as the asset recovers from it's 'oversold' position.

For most of us, therefore, our FONMM and FOLM are desperately unhelpful when it comes to making money from investing. But this needn't be the case. Just imagine if we could reverse the timing of when we feel them - experiencing FOLM when the relevant market is at or close to peaking and FONMM when it's at or close to the bottom. We would have a much better chance of achieving a good return. So how do we go about doing this?

When we experience FONMM, we need to pause and consciously appraise the investment from a FOLM perspective. We could ask ourselves questions such 'What's the chance that the price could reverse sharply? Are there still good fundamental reasons to own the asset? Has the price risen too much, too soon?' Similarly, when prices are falling sharply and FOLM is dominant we need to summon our FONMM. 'Is this investment getting cheap? Have most people got out of it now? Is the price likely to be higher in 12 months than it is now?'

What other people say and do remains influential but in completely the opposite way to before. Instead of thinking 'I must copy what they're doing' we should consider whether it would be better to do the reverse. If, with solid reasons in mind, we determine that this is not the moment, then fair enough. But we also need to be aware that there *will* come a time when it's highly beneficial to resist our natural inclinations and go *against* the crowd. We can listen to the views of market 'experts' as well, but should do so with a healthy dollop of scepticism. As I pointed out, they too can get caught up in the general tide of enthusiasm or gloom, while vested interests will sometimes cloud their judgement.

As well as keeping tabs on our own and other's FONMM and FOLM, we need to be alert for additional, classic signs of bubbles and bottoms. Alarm bells should ring when we hear analysts struggling to explain current valuations or simply not bothering to do so, slipping in words such as 'belief,' 'faith' and 'trust' instead. We should be even more wary if the asset price starts to move exponentially either upwards or downwards. This usually occurs when euphoria or 'end of the world' despondency sets in, both of which can signal that a turning point is nigh. More prosaically, caution is warranted when we find ourselves setting up a simple spreadsheet designed to measure our mounting riches which we update (too) frequently...at least when the price of our investment(s) is rising!

I strongly suggest the actions of major Central Banks are worth watching closely. Asset price bubbles are often popped by rising interest rates (or the anticipation of such) and can form when rates are cut aggressively.

Even with all this in mind, picking the exact top and bottom of an asset price requires more luck than judgement and is *impossible* to do consistently. Just because somebody else tells us that they have achieved it before, does not mean that they will be able to do it again. As such, we shouldn't panic if the market moves against us for a while. Equally, however, we don't want to hold on to an asset for too long, losing the majority of our stake. Most professionals deal with this dilemma by operating a 'stop-loss', selling some or all of the asset they hold if it falls by a certain amount. Similarly, we could establish a 'stop-gain' when prices are rising.

Given the difficulties involved in pinpointing the best time to buy, financial advisors typically suggest that we do something called 'dollar-cost averaging'. That is purchase the same dollar (sterling, euro or whatever) amount of an asset at predetermined intervals - usually monthly or quarterly - irrespective of the prevailing price of the asset. In this way, we buy relatively small amounts of the asset at a range of different price points. The technique has the advantage of removing a lot of stress from our investment decisions and will generally work to our advantage over the 'long term'. But it's not without risks. The price of the asset will need to trend higher during the period we're willing to hold it for if we're going to enjoy profits. Have a look at the two charts below.

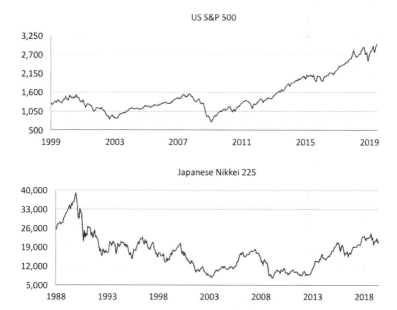

The first shows the US S&P 500 Equity Market Index. Between 1999 and 2012 we would have been lucky to see a positive return using this strategy, but if we had held our nerve and continued investing we would be feeling much happier now. The second tracks the Japanese Nikkei Equity Price Index. Most investors who started regularly buying Japanese shares at virtually *any point* between the late-1980s and 2013 will still be in the red now (not accounting for exchange rate movements or dividends). These experiences, involving two of the world's largest markets, illustrate that we may have to wait years, possibly decades, to experience gains even with a more cautious investment strategy. It emphasises the importance of spreading risks by buying a range of different assets.

Better benchmarking

When judging the performance of our investments, hopefully not more than once or twice a year, we frequently adopt a very simple rule of thumb - if it has fallen that's bad and if it's risen by a reasonable amount that's good. In effect, we compare the change in the price of the asset with zero - feeling disappointed and inclined to sell when it's below the line but happy and tempted to buy more when it's above. Unfortunately, it's a method that's unlikely to serve us well.

Although it won't feel like it, there are occasions when losing money on an investment is far from a failure and gaining money is not a success. Let's say we own shares in several large UK companies, the total value of which has fallen by 5% since we bought them 12 months previously. If the market as a whole has dropped 15% over the same time, we have outperformed. If, however, our portfolio has *risen* by 5% while the market is up 15% we have underperformed and should feel dissatisfied.

Rather than compare the performance of our investments with the zero line it's better to benchmark them with the 'appropriate' market. Admittedly, what counts as appropriate is itself a matter of judgement. Given that, in theory, we could have used the money we spent on shares to buy a government bond, which would have paid us, say, 1.5% interest, our 5% loss should perhaps be compared with a potential 2% gain. But this is to compare apples with oranges given the relative risks involved in investing in these two markets. Having decided to buy shares rather than government bonds we have implicitly signed up to a higher level of risk - that is higher volatility in the price of the asset. As such, we should benchmark the performance of our shares with the wider equity market - the FTSE 100 Index for example - which carries a broadly equivalent level of risk. Over the 'long term' we are likely to be rewarded for holding relatively risky assets by receiving a relatively high return.

Another common mistake when comparing the performance of assets across countries is to forget about exchange rate effects. If, for example, we have purchased an investment vehicle that mirrors the FTSE 100 and it has risen 5%, while the US S&P 500 is up 10% we might conclude that we've done badly. But what if we're a sterling investor and the currency had appreciated by 6% against the US dollar over the same period? Purchasing UK shares was the better investment. Even if it was the dollar that had risen against sterling rather than vice versa we shouldn't necessarily conclude that we made a big mistake. By investing in foreign shares, we're not just gambling on how the underlying asset will perform but what the exchange rate will do as well – we'll be taking an additional risk. While there is nothing necessarily wrong with this, we should at least be aware of it.

So, having benchmarked more appropriately and ascertained how our investments have performed on this basis, how should we react? Do we automatically sell those that have done relatively poorly and buy more of the outperformers?

No! One thing we learnt in the previous section was that our chances of investment success are generally improved by doing the opposite of what comes naturally to us. In the current context, this means thinking about buying more of the underperforming assets and selling the outperforming ones. To be clear, I'm not suggesting that we *necessarily* do this but rather that our first thought is the reverse of what it used to be. Of the relatively poor investment, we ask ourselves, 'Will it continue to underperform or is it getting quite cheap? Is there a catalyst that could turn it around shortly?' And of the outperforming investment, 'Is it too expensive and vulnerable to set back now?'

I suspect that when we're trying to predict the future and the future is very uncertain, which is true of asset prices, we tend to reach for the easy answer - the future will be the like the past. In other words, we assume that our underperforming and outperforming investments will carry on underperforming and outperforming.

When reviewing our investments we also need to consider whether they still fit with what we want them to achieve. Changing circumstances will often require us to change our investment strategy as well. It may be, for instance, that we're intending to retire fairly soon, having built up an adequate nest egg. In this case we should be looking to reduce the riskiness of our portfolio, locking in the gains we've made. Or perhaps we've come into some money which we're willing and can afford to lose. We could opt to invest it in something relatively risky, hoping to be rewarded with a comparatively large return.

Lies, damned lies and charts

We often look at charts as a quick and easy method to determine which assets to buy and sell, generally comparing the current situation with the past to draw implications for the future. There are several issues to be wary of in so doing.

Glancing at the first chart overleaf, which tracks the FTSE 100 Index between January 2006 and September 2007, it's hard to be anything other than optimistic. The Index looks poised to rise further.

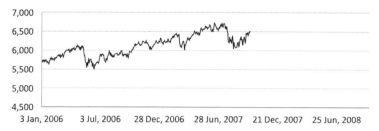

FTSE 100

FTSE 100

The reality, as shown by the bottom graph, is very different, however. It soon slumped. A pattern of rising highs and lows is generally what we look for in the price of an asset to be positive about it, although clearly it's not always a perfect guide. This is just one example of how historical price developments can easily mislead but the lesson is clear - we shouldn't base an investment decision entirely on a simple extrapolation of past developments.

Charts can easily mislead for other reasons as well. The first graph overleaf shows the Year to Date (YTD) performance of the FTSE 100 at the time of writing - it was up by a seemingly impressive 8% in the first seven months of 2019. We are likely to gain a different impression of how good this really is, however, by looking at the Index since the beginning of 2018 - the next chart. This shows that it has yet to fully recover the losses it made during that year.

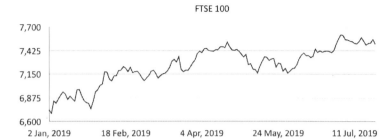

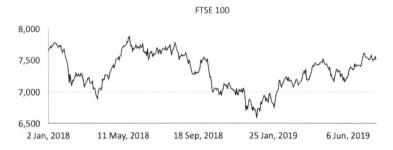

Most charting tools allow us to alter the time horizon and we should use this function as opposed to simply accepting the default period presented to us. It will only add a few seconds to our research time but could make a big difference to the conclusions we reach.

We also need to be careful when looking at long-term price performance charts of assets that have a distinct upward or downward trend. The lines in the charts overleaf are very different even though both track the US S&P 500 Index since 1925. While the first one shows the development of the index in its traditional form, the line in the next one is the natural log of the same series. The latter has the effect of making everything proportionate, so that the 1930s crash looks far larger in this chart than the other, where it's not even visible, and the run up in the index over recent years a lot smaller. Taking logs is the more accurate way of judging historical developments.

S&P 500

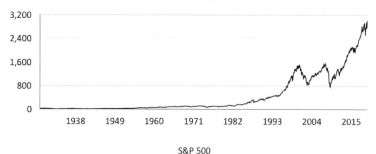

S&P 500

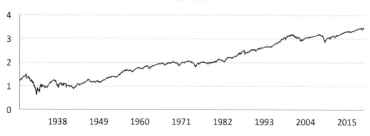

Another, better known, charting distortion is to use misleading scales. If we're not careful we can end up concluding that a relatively small change in the price of an asset is quite large and vice versa, leading us to respectively overplay and underplay the importance of past movements. When viewing a chart, be sure to check that the scales are sensible.

Given how easy it is to fall into these various chart related traps by ourselves, think about how much fun those attempting to persuade us to do certain things, such as buying a particular investment, can have using these tricks.

The uncertainty myth

As an economist for many years I spent a lot of time listening to asset managers whose job it was to invest millions of pounds on their clients' behalf. If I was given one pound every time I heard them suggest that they were waiting for 'greater clarity', or words to that effect, before determining what to do, I would be sitting on a tidy sum myself!

The fact is uncertainty is certain. When one uncertainty is removed others tend to surface. Let's say that ahead of an impending general election we're unsure what the make-up of the next government will be and are reluctant to invest until the result is known. Once it is, however, we might start to concern ourselves with what the new government will do and how long it will last. There's always going to be something to worry about, giving us reason to delay our investment decision if we so choose.

As described to us in 2002 by Donald Rumsfeld, the then US Secretary of Defense, there are two main forms of uncertainty - 'known unknowns' and 'unknown unknowns'. The former relate to things we know exist but do not have all the information about, such as a forthcoming plebiscite or how Brexit will ultimately play out. The latter are events we can't predict or even plan for, including when and where the next natural disaster will strike and what the big inventions of the coming 20 years will be. I suspect that the unpredictable, random nature of 'unknown unknowns' is another reason why we expect uncertainty to diminish in the future. We effectively assume that they won't occur.

Asset markets handle 'known unknowns' by implicitly attaching probabilities to the possible outcomes. Asset prices move to 'price in' changes in these probabilities, with the adjustments coming almost instantaneously when the asset is actively traded. This has important consequences for the way we should invest. Continuing with my general election example, let's say that having waited for the result we decide to buy an asset which we expect to be helped by the new government's policies. If the market has taken the same view as us about that asset, our perceived investment opportunity will have long since gone. In short, if we wait for clarity we'll have waited too long.

The only chance we have of making money in these circumstances is to hold a different view to the market. For instance, we might decide that one Party has a higher chance of winning the election than is generally assumed or the policies of the Party that most people expect to triumph will benefit particular assets to a greater extent than is widely expected. *If* we're right or the market comes round to our way of thinking before the result is known, the prices of the relevant assets will adjust to our financial advantage. Ironically, therefore, we should welcome 'known unknowns' as investors. If the future was entirely certain we couldn't make a capital gain (or loss) as everything would be priced in before we had the opportunity to act.

By contrast, 'unknown unknowns' can't be assessed by markets, meaning that it's only when they play out that asset prices react and, often, violently so. In financial market circles, such events are more commonly termed 'Black Swans', as popularised by Nassim Taleb in his 2007 book:[1] the relevance of black swans being that only white swans were thought to exist until a black swan was seen. He suggested that the best way of dealing with the huge impact such events can have is to adopt a very specific investment strategy. We should avoid 'medium-risk' assets, including equities, and invest 85-90% of our money in the safest possible instruments, such as developed-country government bonds. We use the remainder of our funds to bet on something extraordinary happening.

The main difficulty with this, of course, is determining which assets will be affected and in what direction by the appearance of a Black Swan. Luck will inevitably play a large part, although I guess we 'only' need to be fortuitous once or twice to make a good return. A different way of acting on Taleb's observations is to be nervous when uncertainty - as measured by the volatility of asset prices - is unusually low. Although we can't be sure what will materialise to cause volatility to increase we can be reasonably confident that something will. It's possible to monitor and even 'trade' (buy and sell) volatility in several different asset markets.

Hindsight bias

As well as expecting the future to be less uncertain than the present, we also tend to believe it was easier to invest successfully in the past than it is currently. In other words the toughest time to decide what to do is always right now!

Hindsight bias sees us perceive historical events as more predictable than they were before they took place. We underplay past uncertainties relative to current ones. 'It was obvious the oil price was going to fall sharply having reached such a high level, but what happens next is anybody's guess' or 'sterling was bound to appreciate last year, although I'm not sure which way it will go now' are examples of the way many of us think.

In truth, investing in risky assets has never been easy and never will be. It's important to keep this in mind, not so that it dissuades us from ever putting money in the markets again but rather to make us focus on the here and now: to make a decision rather than to postpone it. Our choice *could* be to wait for a better opportunity, but that's very different from deciding to sit on our hands in anticipation of calmer, less uncertain times when investing was as easy as it was in the past. Sadly, that time will never come.

The incomparability of losses and gains

We dislike losses on our investments as much as we enjoy equivalent sized gains, correct? Although logic dictates that this should be right, many have shown that losing money is psychologically far more painful compared to the pleasure we receive from gaining it. Foremost amongst those is Nobel Laureate Daniel Kahneman who argued, on the basis of empirical investigation, that, '*For most people, the fear of losing $100 (on the toss of a coin) is more intense than the hope of gaining $150.*'[2] It's suggested that our aversion to loss has an evolutionary explanation - we have a better chance of surviving by treating threats as more important than opportunities. This natural human tendency is again generally unhelpful when it comes to investing money, however.

Several experiments have found that our average 'loss aversion ratio' - the smallest gain people are willing to accept to risk the equal chance of losing a given amount of money - is normally 1.5 to 2.5 times the potential loss. The ratio tends to be bigger the higher the stakes that are involved: we're more risk averse when there is a chance of losing £5,000 relative to £500 even if the former is only a small proportion of our wealth.

By implication, therefore, most of us need to be *extremely* confident of profiting from an investment where we could potentially lose money, before being prepared to commit the funds. As a result, we're generally inclined to avoid risky investments in the stock market for example, while favouring much safer vehicles such as high-street banks' deposit accounts. This is a very different approach from that of a trader whose job it is to take risks and who, as a consequence, will have a loss aversion ratio much closer to one.

I'm not suggesting that we suddenly adopt a trader's mentality, but many of us can afford to take more risks when investing than we currently do. A word of warning though. As I pointed out earlier, we're currently most likely to lower our tolerance to risk precisely when we *should* be at our most wary. It's only when we're able to manage our FOLM and FONMM in the ways described in this chapter, that we should countenance investing in riskier assets.

There's one other issue to be aware of when it comes to how we think (differently) about losses and gains. Having made a gain we generally feel inclined to lock it in, while when we have lost money we're more willing to repeat the gamble.

Ironically, our aversion to loss makes us want to 'double up' with the explicit aim of recovering the money we've lost. This is *not* a good reason to invest. It's one thing to buy the same asset again having decided that there are still genuinely strong, fundamental reasons to do so. But if our conclusion is the opposite we must mentally write off the initial investment as a mistake and move on rather than 'chasing the pot'. Each investment decision we make should be independent of whether we previously gained or lost.

In brief

The comparisons we make when investing probably create more problems than any other aspect of our comparison-packed lives. FONMM often leads us to invest when we shouldn't, while FOLM keeps us out of the market when we should be in. We reach the wrong conclusions about the quality of our investments by comparing their returns with zero when we need to use a more appropriate benchmark. We extrapolate past price movements into the future and make all sorts of other charting mistakes when deciding which assets to buy, hold and sell. We expect the future to offer greater clarity than the past when it rarely does. And we treat losses very differently to gains, leading us to be excessively cautious at times.

Rather than ignore what our instincts are telling us to do, we should use them as triggers to at least consider doing the precise opposite! More generally, being aware of the problems our comparisons can cause and making more appropriate ones will generate better outcomes. This is true both financially and, as we have discovered throughout this book, in a *huge* variety of other circumstances. As such, it's not a bad thought to end on.

References

Introduction

[1] Gerber, J.P., Wheeler, L., & Suls, J. (2018). A social comparison theory meta-analysis 60+ years on. *Psychological Bulletin, 144*(2), 177-197.

[2] Maltz, M. (1960). *Psycho-Cybernetics*. Englewood Cliffs, NJ: Prentice-Hall.

Chapter 1

[1] Wood, J.V. (1996). What is social comparison and how should we study it? *Personality and Social Psychology Bulletin, 22*, 520-537.

[2] Festinger, L. (1954). A theory of social comparison processes. *Human Relations, 7*, 117-140.

[3] Corcoran, K., Crusius, J., & Mussweiler, T. (2011). Social comparisons: Motives, standards and mechanisms. In D. Chadee (Ed.), *Theories in Social Psychology* (pp.119-139). Oxford, UK: Wiley-Blackwell.

Chapter 2

[1] Adler, A. (1964). *Problems of Neurosis: A Book of Case Histories*. P. Mairet (Ed.). New York, NY: Harper & Row.

[2] Rohrer, J.M., Egloff, B., & Schmukle, C. (2015). Examining the effects of birth order on personality. *Proceedings of the National Academy of Sciences, 112*(46), 14224-14229.

[3] Damian, R.L., & Roberts, B.W. (2015). The associations of birth order with personality and intelligence in a representative sample of US high school students. *Journal of Research in Personality, 58*, 96-105.

[4] Falbo, T., & Polit, D. (1986). Quantitative review of the only child literature: Research evidence and theory development. *Psychological Bulletin,100*(2), 176-189.

[5] Tesser, A. (1988). Towards a self evaluation maintenance model of social behaviour. In L. Berkowitz (Ed.), *Advances in Experimental Social Psychology* (Vol. 21, pp 181-227). New York, NY: Academic Press.

[6] Huguet, P., Carlier, M., Dolan, C.V., de Geus, E.J., & Boomsma, D.I. (2017). Social comparison orientation in monozygotic and dizygotic twins. *Twin Research and Human Genetics, 20*(6), 550-557.

[7] Falbo, T. (1981). Relationships between birth category, achievement, and interpersonal orientation. *Journal of Personality and Social Psychology, 41*(1), 121-131.

[8] Meunier, J.C, Roskam, I., Stievenart, M., van de Moortele, G., Browne, D.T., & Wade, M. (2012). Parental differential treatment, child's externalizing behaviour and sibling relationships. *Journal of Social and Personal Relationships, 29*(5), 612-638.

[9] Zervas, L.J., & Sherman, M.F. (1994). The relationship between perceived parental favoritism and self-esteem. *Journal of Genetic Psychology, 155*(1), 25-33.

[10] Sanders, G.S., & Suls, J. (1982). Social Comparison, Competition and Marriage. *Journal of Marriage and Family, 44*(3), 721-730.

[11] Bertrand, M., Kamenica, E., & Pan, J. (2015). Gender identity and relative income within households. *Quarterly Journal of Economics, 2*, 571-614.

[12] Schwartz, C.R., & Gonalons-Pons, P. (2016). Trends in relative earnings and marital dissolution: Are wives who outearn their husbands still more likely to divorce? *Journal of the Social Sciences, 2*(4) 218-236.

[13] Dijkstra, P., Kuyper, H., van der Werf, G., Buunk, A.P., & van der Zee, Y.G. (2008). Social comparisons in the classroom: A review. *Review of Educational Research, 78*(4), 828-879.

[14] Blanton, H., Buunk, B.P., Gibbons, F.X., & Kuyper, H. (1999). When better-than-others compare upward: Choice of comparison and comparative evaluation as independent predictors of academic performance. *Journal of Personality and Social Psychology, 76*(3), 420-430.

[15] Brown, D.J., Ferris, D.L., Heller, D., & Keeping, L.M. (2007). Antecedents and consequences of the frequency of upward and downward social comparisons at work. *Organizational Behavior and Human Decision Processes 102*, 59-75.

[16] Cohn, A., Fehr, E., Herrmann, B., & Schneider, F. (2011). Social Comparison in the Workplace: Evidence from a Field Experiment. *University of Zurich, Working Paper 7.*

Chapter 3

[1] Twenge, J.M., Martin, G.N., & Campbell, W.K. (2018). Decreases in psychological well-being among American adolescents after 2012 and links to screen time during the rise of smartphone technology. *Emotion*. Advance online publication.

[2] Forest, A.M., & Wood, J.V. (2012). When social networking is not working: Individuals with low self-esteem recognize but do not reap the benefits of self-disclosure on Facebook. *Psychological Science, 23*, 295-302.

[3] Tromholt, M. (2016). The Facebook experiment: Quitting Facebook leads to higher levels of well-being. *Cyberpsychology Behavior and Social Networking, 19*(11), 661-666.

[4] Kross, E., Verduyn, P., Demiralp, Park, J., Lee, D.S., Lin.N., Shablack, H., Jonides, J., & Ybarra, O. (2013). Facebook use predicts declines in subjective well-being in young adults. *PLoS ONE, 8*(8), e69841.

[5] Hunt, M.G., Marx, R., Lipson, C., & Young, J. (2018) No more FOMO: Limiting social media decreases loneliness and depression. *Journal of Social and Clinical Psychology, 37*(10), 751-768.

[6] Przybylski, A.K., & Weinstein, N. (2017). A large-scale test of the goldilocks hypothesis: Quantifying the relations between digital-screen use and the mental well-being of adolescents. *Psychological Science*, *28*(2), 204-215.

[7] Kuss, D., & Griffiths, M.D. (2017). Social networking sites and addiction: Ten lessons learned. I*nternational Journal of Environmental Research and Public Health, 14*(3), 311.

[8] Jenner, F. (2015). At least 5% of young people suffer symptoms of social media addiction. Available from: https://horizon-magazine.eu/article/least-5-young-people-suffer-symptoms-social-media-addiction.html. Accessed October 2018.

[9] Chou, C., & Edge, N. (2012). "They are happier and having better lives than I am": The impact of using Facebook on perceptions of others' lives. *Cyberpsychology, Behaviour and Social Networking, 15*(2), 117-21.

[10] Feinstein, B.A., Hershenberg, R. Bhatia, V., Latack, J.A, Meuwly, N., & Davila, J. (2013). Negative social comparison on Facebook and depressive symptoms: Rumination as a mechanism. *Psychology of Popular Media Culture 2*(3), 161-170.

[11] Vogel, E., Rose, J.P., & Roberts, L. (2014). Social comparison, social media, and self-esteem. *Psychology of Popular Media Culture, 3*(4) 206-222.

[12] Fardouly, J., Diedrichs, P.C., Vartanian, L.R., & Halliwell, E. (2015). Social comparisons on social media: The impact of Facebook on young women's body image concerns and mood. *Body Image, 13*, 38-45.

[13] Myers, T., & Crowther, J. (2009). Social comparison as a predictor of body dissatisfaction: A meta-analytic review. *Journal of Abnormal Psychology, 118*, 683-698.

[14] Wolke, D., Lee, K., & Guy, A. (2017). Cyberbullying: a storm in a teacup? *European Child & Adolescent Psychiatry*, *26*(8), 899-908.

Chapter 5

[1] White, J.B., Langer, E.J., Yariv, L., Welch IV, J.C. (2006). Frequent social comparisons and destructive emotions and behaviours: The dark side of social comparisons. *Journal of Adult Development, 13*(1), 36-44.

Chapter 8

[1] Townsend, S.S.M., Kim, H.S., & Mesquita, B. (2014). Are you feeling what I'm feeling? Emotional similarity buffers stress. *Social Psychological and Personality Science*, *5*(5) 526-533.

[2] Saanijoki, T., Tuominen, L., Tuulari, J., Nummenmaa, L., Arponon, E., Kalliokoski, K., & Hirvonen, J. (2018). Opioid release after high-intensity interval training in healthy human subjects. *Neuropsychopharmacology 43*(2), 246-254.

Chapter 9

[1] Duhigg, C. (2013). *The Power of Habit*. London, UK: Random House Books.

Chapter 12

[1] Ariely, D. (2010). *Predictably Irrational*. New York, NY: Harper Collins.

Chapter 13

[1] Moore, D.A. (2007). When good = better than average. *Judgment and Decision Making, 2*(5), 277-291.

[2] Shinar, D., & Compton, R. (2004). Aggressive driving: An observational study of driver, vehicle and situational variables. *Accident Analysis & Prevention, 36*(3), 429-437.

[3] Jann. B. (2002). Driver aggression as a function of status concurrency: An analysis of horn-honking responses. *University of Bern research report*.

[4] Finkel, E.J., Eastwick, P.W., Karney, B.R., Reis, H.T., & Sprecher, S. (2012). Online dating: A critical analysis from the perspective of psychological science. *Psychological Science in the Public Interest, 13*(1), 3-66.

Chapter 14

[1] Frey, B.S, Meier, S. (2004). Social comparisons and pro-social behaviour. Testing 'conditional cooperation' in a field experiment. *The American Economic Review, 94*(5), 1717-1722.

[2] Iyengar, S.S., Jiang, W., & Humberman, G., (2004). How much choice is too much? Contributions to 401 (k) retirement plans. In O.S. Mitchell & S.P. Utkus (Eds.) *Pension Design and Structure: New Lessons from Behavioural Finance* (pp.83-96). New York, NY: Oxford University Press.

[3] Dellot, B., & Wallace-Stephens, F. (2017). The age of automation. Artificial intelligence, robotics and the future of low-skilled work. *RSA Action and Research Centre*.

[4] Evans, L., & Kitchen, R. (2018). A smart place to work? Big data systems, labour and modern retail stores. *New Technology, Work and Employment, 33*(1), 44-57.

[5] Dunn, J., Ruedy, N.E., & Schweitzer, M.E. (2012). It hurts both ways: How social comparisons harm affective and cognitive trust. *Organizational Behavior and Human Decision Processes 107*, 2-14.

[6] Arnone, M., & Stumpf, S.A. (2010). Shared leadership: From rivals to co-CEOs. *Strategy and Leadership 38*(2):15-21.

Chapter 16

[1] Taleb, N. (2007). *The Black Swan: The Impact of the Highly Improbable*. New York, NY: Random House.

[2] Kahneman, D. (2012). *Thinking Fast and Slow*. London, UK: Penguin Group.

Printed in Great Britain
by Amazon